To: Arde

MW00427144

Spiritual Storytelling
and the
Mysterious
Young Child

From:
Sharlet g Mc Clurkin

May God bless & lead
you in your life!

June 9, 2022

Spiritual Storytelling and the *Mysterious* Young Child

Sharlet McClurkin

Learn how using simple Bible figures can open
a young child's heart to know God

Spiritual Storytelling and the Mysterious Young Child

Trilogy Christian Publishers A Wholly Owned Subsidiary of Trinity Broadcasting Network
2442 Michelle Drive Tustin, CA 92780

Rights Department, 2442 Michelle Drive, Tustin, CA 92780.
Trilogy Christian Publishing/TBN and colophon are trademarks of Trinity Broadcasting Network.

Cover design by: Christina Hicks

For information about special discounts for bulk purchases, please contact Trilogy Christian Publishing.

Trilogy Disclaimer: The views and content expressed in this book are those of the author and may not necessarily reflect the views and doctrine of Trilogy Christian Publishing or the Trinity Broadcasting Network. Manufactured in the United States of America

10 9 8 7 6 5 4 3 2 1

Library of Congress Cataloging-in-Publication Data is available.

ISBN: 978-1-63769-626-2

E-ISBN: 978-1-63769-627-9

Dedication

"A little child shall lead them."

I dedicate this book to the young children of the world who have taught me so much. I thank God for teaching me to observe young children as my calling, joy, and privilege. My Lord Jesus Christ taught me to look perpetually and faithfully each day for the best within children; to love and enjoy them as He does; to humbly apologize when I am wrong, and to cling to the eternal hope, along with them, even though they don't know it yet and I have not named it for them, that they will be able to reach their full potential in their lifetime.

Acknowledgments

Thank you to my third granddaughter, Brooke McClurkin, who typed and edited this book, to Teiya McClurkin, my second granddaughter, for gathering pictures from my computer, and to Angela S, my church friend who became inspired by seeing the Child and Faith lessons in a workshop a few years ago. She encouraged me in meeting the challenges of finalizing this book and counseled me. My greatest contributor, of course, was my husband, Donald, who died five years ago. Still, without him, I would not have had the courage to attend the Cavalletti workshop and to have been able to fill suitcases with Christian materials, to get through Chinese customs, and to travel to China for nearly thirty years as well as to Viet Nam for five years. In our first full-time class in 2007, we carried as many Chinese Bibles as we could to distribute secretly to students and conferees. When leaving our hotel, I left a Chinese Bible under the bed pillow for the hotel housekeeper, but she ran out with it to the check-out counter, yelling something about my leaving it! Nothing happened. Soon we found Christian students who could go to Christian bookstores and purchase enough Bibles for the entire class of about thirty students each year.

Because students wanted to sit on the front rows, they all came early and attended the optional Bible lessons with figures. Once, I had just given the lesson on The Ten Secrets to a Happy Life, and an older Chinese woman raised her hand and asked, "Why do I need to hear this lesson? I am a Communist."

I replied, "All of these lessons are optional, but I believe that God created you and loves you. You may not know it yet, but He wanted you to hear this story about how to be happy in life." Even students who did not become Christians told us later that the peace of God and hope for the future rose within them when they heard the stories.

Donald carried suitcases up many stairs and down again. He organized shelves of learning materials and Child and Faith lessons while I spoke, and I did the same for him. We were a team with equal status between us who encouraged one another and observed and learned about Chinese culture together. One Taiwanese professor said to me, "Sharlet, the students don't care much about what you say regarding Donald or about God, or what Donald says about you! What they see and remember is how he treats you! They say he treats you like a queen!"

Table of Contents

Foreword

I fully intended to become an inspirational professor of humanities, to awaken the "blank slate" of college freshmen to the beautiful unfolding of creativity and greatness of ideas found within humanity, especially as expressed in US Documents of Independence, Greek culture, and the Renaissance. It was fitting that, after the death of my father in World War II, I received a full National Defense Education Act fellowship for a three-year PhD degree in a program at Florida State University. I have yet to discover how this Education Act came about, but I entered graduate school with a strong foundation in ancient history and philosophy.

This was the second miraculous educational intervention in my life. The first had been created by the superintendent of schools, Mr. Whitman, in Topeka, Kansas, in 1948, with his innovative program for a special "guinea pig" class of thirty gifted children. We were graduates from elementary schools all over Topeka and would be tested and selected for an intensive three-year junior high program in language, math, history, and geometry. (I can still remember what most of the IQ questions were that they asked me when I was eleven years old.) Some of us had already had two years in the study of Latin at the old Quinton Heights Elementary School, due to our principal, Ms. Snell. Mr. Whitman had also set up a city-wide Suzuki-violin music program the previous year, but parents could not stand the squalling sound of violin practice at home. We all got to take home small violins!

Thirty of us took public busses to the wealthy west-side Boswell Junior High. There I encountered expensive clothing, such as angora sweaters, one for each day of the week, and the daughter of our governor who had not been selected for the special class. I also noticed several other girls besides myself with poor clothing, one of whom was black and died of a brain tumor that year. As a twelve-year-old child, I reached out to her in friendship and prayed for God to heal her; I was very sad when she passed away. Death had touched my life once again, but now I was reading the comforting words of Jesus each night. The other girl, Judith, and I became study partners for three years during recesses as well as consultants to each other in how to get the best grades. We were the top two in the class.

Friday was the day that each student had to present a five-minute speech to the entire class. I had a terrible fear of anyone finding out about my turbulent home life, and I had a monstrous blushing and sweating problem. My so-called friend, Kaye M., made up a poem about me:

"Scarlet Sharlet gets so red she looks like a red beet head!"

Imagine thirty smart-aleck children listening to your weekly speech! Laughter at me would have been a frightening blow to my ego, but it only happened once.

A few weeks after school began, I gave my third speech, and the boy in front of me, Victor G., turned around and said, "Why do you always talk about dogs or picnics?"

I had the nerve to say to him, "I don't like you."

And he replied, "The feeling is mutual!" I had to look up what that meant. After Victor criticized me, I made up a fairy tale with a heroine named Penelope. When I gave the speech, I mispronounced the heroine's name, and everyone laughed. I had never heard the name spoken and did not know that the emphasis is on the second syllable. When we all left for the huge Topeka High School in 1951, most of the gifted children remained together in Latin, English, and Geometry. There was never any accountability for the gifted program, whether it worked or what the outcomes could have been.

In 1959 or before, the Federal Government created the NDEA program to foster an interest in the foundational philosophies of our country. I left my pre-med program after my junior year and finished the four years of college by experiencing new areas of learning with such non-scientific topics as economics, sociology, physics, and being the editor of the college newspaper. I took my third year of two-week choir trips around the United States and enjoyed becoming the soloist that year.

After one year of studying humanities at FSU, I was disappointed in the overbearing emphasis of the program on humanism, as well as the rejection of any appreciation of God's marvelous and multitudinous gifts to humankind and their expression in culture. Tearing down the Christian faith was my professor's main interest in each class. My brother, Alan, received the same NDEA fellowship the following year and had the courage to debate the professor in class. My best friend and pastor back in Kansas asked me to marry him, so I gave up the program and began helping my husband with choir, college-age Bible studies, and making drapes for our new house. We had our daughter, Sharron, that year, with whom I now live in retirement.

I was hired as an instructor for the required humanities year of history classes at the local university in Topeka. Here I discovered how much I love to teach and that I enjoy creating non-traditional methods to communicate concepts to human beings, whatever age they are: dramas, debates, what-ifs...The only education course that I took in college was history of education, where I read one page about Maria Montessori.

When we moved to Atlanta in 1963 for Donald to pursue a master's degree in Christian education, I was hired to a college history teaching position and, once again, enjoyed challenging the students to think. In both universities, I had several students tell me that they were going to change their major to history.

After we moved to a church in Seattle in 1968, a friend told Donald that we should enroll our two-and-a-half-year-old son in the Montessori school near Sea-Tac Airport. I took him there, and he never looked back; he just took his banana to cut and walked in. He began trying to make friends by pushing other children! I started reading Dr. Maria Montessori's *The Secret of Childhood* and other books, and my life changed. I have spent fifty years trying to understand and learn from young children from her profound writings. Then I began seeking to find God's character and nature not only in the Word of God but in His beautiful creation, the young child.

Introduction

The fax machine was crackling, and I was reaping the results of faxing schools in various countries. The phone was also within hearing distance of my bed. It rang at three a.m., and someone said, "Borneo here! Can you come to teach us about Montessori education?" It was 1988, and I had been praying for eight years for an open door to teach in Asia. God was pushing me to knock on doors and to follow Him. My heart was crying out for His will.

Finally, a US student in our Montessori training class gave me a name and fax number of a prominent Montessori school in Tainan, Taiwan. By faith, I faxed her saying that we would be visiting her school in October and would be available to begin a training program there. When I called the school, I heard the American folk song "Old Black Joe" playing in the background in English! I spoke with the director who invited us to train thirty teachers for their schools, to begin in a few weeks. We negotiated a plan and were on our way! For three years, we gave the course there, meeting many duplicitous but exciting challenges, as well as wonderful teachers. Soon, the teachers were coming to the US for summer courses, from fifty to sixty teachers at a time. We rented apartments in Kent, Washington, and Donald filled them with sleeping bags, cookware, and dishes for six-week-long courses.

My old secretary at our school in the US gave me her friend's phone number to call when I arrived at Tainan, which I did. Her Taiwanese pastor/husband gave me the phone number of his sister, a professor of Piaget in a university in Taipei. That led us to another professor, William, in a Presbyterian

Seminary in Hsinchu, who invited us to speak to nearly 1,000 Buddhist teachers there. I was able to give the story "The Announcement to the Shepherds" on an overhead screen to them. William invited us to a Chinese breakfast at six a.m. unexpectedly one morning. We met Christian seminary professors from South Korea who gave our information to a pastor's wife in Taejon, South Korea. We met her and began traveling around South Korea and speaking at universities with Moon, and then with William and his wife to universities in China. One connection led to another, and then another until we ended up speaking and teaching all over China for nearly thirty years. Soon our students were opening doors to many schools in China in various cities. We opened our first full-time course in Beijing in 2007 and our first training course in Viet Nam in 2012. Many of our graduates are now teacher trainers and Christians.

The Coronavirus pandemic has pushed us to create a "modern" Montessori training program that includes many new materials suitable to the cultural needs of young children in early learning. The curriculum which I wrote and refined over thirty years is now available as a "hybrid" course with two-thirds of the course online and one-third onsite. It may be taken in any country with guidelines available to follow for certification by Montessori Teacher Preparation of Washington (Kent, Washington) and the International Association of Progressive Montessori (Grover Beach, California).

Part 1

Chapter 1
How One Teacher, as a Child, Finds God

In October 1943, my father, Anson, was killed by a German tank while swimming across the Volturno River north of Naples, Italy. I was six years old. The Volturno bridge had been blown up by the Germans, so Anson, a gymnast and captain of a US Army company, wore a vest and swam across the river to connect a supply line for his men to proceed north and remove the Germans from Italy. He made it but was shot. I remember the place where I was sitting in our small living room in Topeka, Kansas, and who was in the room: my mother, grandmother, and grandfather, two aunts, and my two brothers, ages four and nine months, when someone brought us a telegram and read it to us: "Leroy Anson Haselwood has been killed." I remember feeling worried about my mother and how she would take this. She was very fragile. I remember wondering why all the women were crying but not my grandfather and four-year-old brother. I wondered what this would mean for us. We had just moved from Kansas City, where I had begun singing and reading and telling time in kindergarten. I wanted to go to the same school I was in now. I did not want to move again.

An unknown person had taught me a prayer to say after I went to bed at night: "Now I lay me down to sleep. I pray the

Lord my soul to keep. If I should die before I wake, I pray the Lord my soul to take."

I would say it with my brother, Alan, every night.

> *"God will take and keep my soul."*

Leroy Anson Haselwood, Wilda, Alan, 3 and Sharlet, nearly 5

It would be some months later that we moved to my grandparents' farm in Gardner, Kansas, and my grandmother Wenger took me, age seven, and my brother, almost six, to the Presbyterian church in town. We sat in a row in the middle of the sanctuary when two lines of adults came walking from the back, down the left aisle in long robes with scarves around their neck, singing, "Holy, holy, holy, Lord God Almighty!" I looked all around the room to find someone who was "holy" but could not find anyone. I was not even sure what that meant, but I thought it was serious. Grandmother never took us again.

> *"God is holy."*

About two years later, after Mother married Sam, and we moved back to Topeka, I remember sitting on a swing in our side yard, looking up at the blue sky and white clouds, on a summer day, and I said, "Dear God, I want to know you. Who are you? Please tell me."

It wasn't long before Mother came to me one Sunday morning and said, "Sharlet, help me get your brothers ready for church today. You can comb their hair," and then she took us to Central Presbyterian Church in Topeka and dropped us off for Sunday school. My brothers were eight and four years of age. One had brown hair, and one had blonde hair. I parted them on the side. At Sunday school, my teacher gave me a Bible and told me to read it, and, another Sunday, she told us to memorize the Ten Commandments and Psalm 1. I did.

My mother only began coming to church years later. She had to keep the house perfectly clean. (In 1960, she prayed with my husband, Donald, to receive Christ.) She grew in her faith through her friends in Al-Anon, the women's organization of Alcoholics Anonymous.

The church was on Huntoon Street, a one-way road, with a church on every corner for about a mile. Mother thought that she was pulling into the Congregational Church, but she pulled into the second corner, after the Church of Science, and it was a Presbyterian church. Were it not for our being late and her mistake, I would never have met my future husband in 1958 in a small Presbyterian church on the west side of town. God marvelously directs our paths.

> *"God is good."*
>
> *"God gave us ten secrets to a happy life."*
>
> *God told us how to be blessed.*
>
> *"God will bless the person who dwells in the house of the Lord and meditates on His Word."*
>
> *"God hears our prayers and answers them."*

I did what my teacher asked me and began my walk of faith at about nine years old.

I believe that someone else was praying for me. I began reading every day, and the Word of God taught me, gave me *courage, self-confidence, peace,* and *happiness,* especially the words of Jesus. Without the Bible reading in my life, I do not think that I could have survived the turbulence in my home. When I read in the gospels that Jesus said to *forgive* "*seventy times seven,*" I began doing that for my step-father's words and actions. After a few years, I realized that it meant to "keep forgiving," not a definite number. But the thought never crossed my mind that I could forgive the Germans for killing my father.

In 1980, Donald and I sold our home, two schools, and most of our belongings and followed God's direction to move to Seattle, Washington. I knew it would make it easier for us to do Montessori training in China from the west coast of the US. We filled the largest Ryder truck available with my piano, Donald's theology books, limited furniture, and the children's and our belongings and left Kansas. My son, Sim, Donald, and I drove the truck, and our two daughters drove our small Isuzu car, and we left for the west coast. As we were pulling away, my husband asked me, "Sharlet, do you think that we are doing the right thing?"

I replied, "Well, if it isn't, it's too late!" God blessed us with a large Montessori school and teacher training in Kent, Washington, a few years later. We drove as far as Abraham walked from Ur to Canaan.

I have always wondered who taught me that night-time

prayer; nevertheless, it had soothed my fears through my early years, even if it dealt with death. Just from that one prayer, I knew there was a God and that He cared for me. He is good. Through those years, I never blamed God for my father's death; I blamed the Germans. I hated them. Not until I was an adult at a swimming pool with my children later in life did I voice my anger to a German family who was loudly enjoying a summer day at a pool in Kansas. I asked the woman why the Germans had killed my father, and she screamed back to me, "Why did you blow up all of our beautiful buildings?"

A few years later, when Donald and I were in Milan, Italy, admiring *The Lord's Supper* by Leonardo Da Vinci, at the cathedral of Santa Maria Dell Gracie, I had an epiphany. After viewing the painting, I was searching for some hand-painted trays at a market outside of the church, and the salesman asked, "Why are you in Italy?"

I answered, "Because my husband thought it might help relieve my sorrow about my father's death by the Germans."

(In my childhood, I had never been allowed to grieve my father's death. We were never allowed to speak of Anson or about him. Sam wanted us to forget about Anson, so we did. But during the Gulf War, as a married woman, I began experiencing deep unhappiness and grief. I could not bear seeing fighting on the news. So my husband, Don, made plans for us to visit Italy.)

The salesman (an Italian) said, "Just one *momento!*", turned to leave, and then came back with a woman. He said, "This is my wife. Her father was killed by those 'blankety-blank' Germans." She looked straight at me without speaking (she knew no English) and stood there, and I looked at her without speaking (I knew little Italian), and we both sobbed.

> *"God allowed my father to be killed, but he died for*
> *a high purpose."*
>
> *"I was a free person who could choose to travel to Italy and find*
> *the river where the battle happened."*

My hatred was gone. Her husband's swear words expressed my feelings exactly. A few years later, Donald and I spent a week in a timeshare south of Munich and enjoyed meeting German people, the food, the countryside, and all of the experiences.

> *"God is good!"*

Chapter 2
Observing God's Image in the Young Child

"Mrs. McClurkin, my goldfish died," four-year-old Jenny told me one day after circle in my Montessori classroom.

I replied in good "active-listening" fashion, "You're very sad."

"Will it go to heaven?" she continued.

What could I say to her? I wondered and slowly replied, "God loves you and all of the creatures that He has made," hoping she would be satisfied with this answer.

Persisting, she asked, "But will I get to see it in heaven?"

"Jenny, I am sorry that I don't know the answer to that, but I do know that Jesus told us His Father knows when any sparrow falls to the ground and how many hairs are on your head. So I know that God cares for all His creatures—everyone."

She said, "Okay," turned quickly, and went to choose her "work" in the classroom. Her strong desire to know God's way, as well as to choose, are part of God's image in her.

"Young children easily receive simple, partial answers and set that information into their brain to be recalled upon later command. It will then be filled in with more mature information."

But I determined to find a more complete answer for her and for other children as soon as I could.

Having been with the young children, ages two and one-half to six, for more than ten years, I felt capable of meeting most of the emotional and learning needs of young children in a basic way, but this was a new question. I had been open to learning how to share my faith in Jesus Christ more specifically to the children than in traditional ways, such as through thanking God for our food, singing simple songs of faith, and praying for children's family members as they shared their needs at circle time first thing in the morning. The Christian teachers and I told Bible stories and celebrated Christmas and Easter, but the wonders of the Word of God were hard to communicate to young children in a meaningful way. One year at our school Christmas program, with teachers, parents, and children, we brought out a large birthday cake for Jesus with lit candles, and suddenly, my second granddaughter, Teiya, spoke out loudly to the whole audience, "When will He be here?"

I answered, "He is in our hearts. He is already here, but we can't just see Him."

Being trained as Montessori teachers, we understood that the youngest children learn best through their five senses. We could not attempt to explain God to young children through traditional, didactic materials or even through music. How could we share the story of God's love with the youngest children? "Just show the children the love of God through your love for them," was what most Christians who had worked with children for years told me. "They can be given more of the Gospel when they are older."

I thought, *That makes sense, but I still am going to open myself to find another way to share God's Word with them.*

Somehow, in the early 1980s, I found the book *Religious Potential of the Child* by Dr. Sofia Cavialetti, read it, and at Christmas experimented with a lesson for children about the announcement to the shepherds. I prepared a tray for the story with four shepherds, a felt, six sheep, and four angels. Trying to replicate the bright light in the sky, I added a penlight. I told the children the story as I moved the figures, as well as turning on the penlight when the angels arrived. The children seemed to enjoy it.

Later, a four-year-old boy took that tray to his floor rug and began to tell himself the story. All seemed to go well until I saw him put the angel on top of the penlight, turn it on, and heard him say, "Ooh. Here comes Luke Skywalker!" At that moment, I experienced a general truth of early childhood that I would confirm later in my experience:

> *"Do not add extraneous materials that might distract the child from the true meaning of the story."*
>
> *"Who knows what theology was created in the child's mind from that lesson?"*
>
> *"The penlight introduced an apparatus that appeals to fantasy, rather than reality, in the shepherd story. Children are very capable of imagining items that they know in their world, such as 'light,' without the penlight."*

In Cavalletti's book, I found many new, interesting concepts, one of which was the example she gave of the profound ability of young children to discern sophisticated concepts through observing the world. She wrote:

> A boy came to his mother one day and asked, "Mother, how did I get here?" and the mother said, "Well, son, many billions of years ago this earth was formed from a gigantic explosion, called the 'big bang.' Many years after that life formed on the earth, including plants, animals, and people. Finally, you were born."

The boy began to laugh and laugh, and said, "No, mother, I don't want to hear a fairy tale! I want to know the truth. How did I get here?" The mother continued to try to convince her son of the veracity of the big bang theory, but he refused to accept it. In the nearly forty years of my giving spiritual stories to the youngest children, I have heard them tell me many profound theological truths that they could never have been taught: They could only intuit the truth. At the young age children may reject the "big-bang theory," but they almost never question the truth of the stories from the Bible.

> "When children hear the simple Bible being read, they never question whether it is a fairy tale. As a preface to its reading, however, we do state, 'This is the Word of God.'"

There is something special within the nature of the young child's heart, soul, mind, and spirit that can be seen and heard in the first four or five years of life. Our Lord told us, "*Unless you become as a little child, you shall not enter the kingdom of heaven*" (Matthew 18:3). This special nature of the youngest child is what this book is about: What is the nature of the young child's being, and does it show us the nature of God Himself? How long does it last in its simplest form, and when does the child finally change to a different way of understanding life?

The other strong concept Sofia explains is the idea of "essentiality." What is the "essence" or one main idea that we want children to understand in our lesson to them? Young children do not want to know nor need to know all the surrounding ideas of one story. Those facts should fall in place later. For now, the essence of the truth is what they want to know. For instance, when I tell young children the story of the Found Son (Prodigal Son), I do not include the jealous older brother's problem that his father forgave his brother. This part of the story is important but can be left out in the first few times it is told so that young children do not get distracted by the family problem. And they will because young children deeply believe in justice and equality. (Most young children will say that the five maidens in the parable of the ten maidens should have shared their oil, and the bridegroom in the parable should have opened the door and let the late maidens in!)

One of Maria Montessori's main functioning concepts is "isolation of difficulty," or the removal of non-essential items from the lesson that the teacher gives the child regarding how to use the special learning materials. Perhaps Sofia gleaned her "essentiality" concept from Maria Montessori, whom she never met, but fashioned her spiritual materials after the Montessori materials. Sofia trusted the child to use the material she made after she told them the story, just as Montessori allowed the children to use the hands-on learning materials after their lesson. It is said that Sofia studied the Montessori theory and admired it. Just as the Montessori teacher may quietly step in and add a missing, necessary part of the use of the learning materials, Sofia allowed the spiritual teacher to do the same. And we can learn to trust that the child will discover the lacking part of the story from the next time she hears it given by a teacher or even another child on the next rug over on the floor.

> *"Children thrive when they are not corrected but are shown 'another' way. We can say, 'Let's try this,' or 'Let me show you,' or just reach out and move the figure and finish telling the story in a gentle way. (If you can, you might say 'May I show you?') The child's self-confidence grows when she believes that she 'can do it.' Children thrive when adults trust them."*

We know that Montessori said, *"Children and adults are at opposite poles of humanity."* An old-time Montessori teacher recently asked me what I think this means (interesting that she was thinking about this again). I replied that Maria wanted us to try to remember how children learn (or learn again by observing the child) so that we can begin to understand them. We adults have forgotten how children think, or what they need, how they love, and why their feelings are so strong. It is because we are now so far apart from what children are like and how they learn, just as far as the north and south poles are from one another. For young children, we must try to understand that they learn differently than we do and try to take into our adult nature some forgotten child-like qualities. These qualities are innocent and pure, God-like qualities, while childish qualities are self-centered and demanding. Young children have both characteristics, of course. Many people have never seen the God-like qualities in young children.

> *"The more humble the adult is, the more she is honored to learn from children yet to realize that, although we adults and the children may learn in different ways, we are all human beings, created by God."*

In 1984 my husband, Donald, and I attended Sofia Cavalletti's Catechesis of the Good Shepherd course in St. Paul, Minnesota, at St. Catherine's College. Since Donald was an ordained Presbyterian pastor, he was allowed into the advanced class of about twenty-five adults with Cavialetti as the teacher, and I was put into Sofia's assistant's class of about thirty Catholic adults. I was introduced to Catechesis concepts with several days of theology and a few lessons. The beginning lesson was the Good Shepherd, and I realized, by soaking in that lesson with my entire soul, that I had found what I was searching for.

My theological education had come from reading the Bible that my Sunday school teacher gave me when I was about nine years old, then eight years of Sunday school, and six years of weekly after-school studies with the pastor of my Presbyterian church and a small group of teenagers when I was in junior and senior high school. When I was thirteen, my parents surprised me with a beautiful upright piano and by granting me piano lessons which I took throughout my high school years. I could not practice enough to become competent in accompanying the youth group in singing hymns; however, I could sing them. Six years of singing and playing praise songs from the Presbyterian Hymnal founded my love and praise for God. I had also taken a required course in the New Testament at my Christian college. I asked more questions than anyone else, which I also did in the Catechesis course.

My mother's brother was our family doctor, and in the summer of 1952, he discovered that I had an unexplained fever. (I am sure that it was from stress. As soon as I left for college, I never had debilitating menstrual cramps again.) The doctor told me to go to bed until the fever came down. He thought that I had rheumatic fever. I did not have any other symptoms, however, and by August, I had decided that no matter what, I would just get up and go anyway to my first year of high school. I returned to church and discovered that there would soon be a week-long high school camp for teenagers in central Kansas. I doubted that Sam would allow Alan and me to go, but he did. (About five years later, Sam prayed with Billy Graham via TV to receive Christ.) The last night of the camp, the old man who was the speaker and a missionary just back from Ethiopia spoke about Jesus Christ, showed us a slide of the Good Shepherd with his sheep, and asked us to stand up if we would like to give our lives to Christ. I did, at age fourteen, and then my brother, Alan, almost thirteen, stood. (My first Sunday school teacher's son, who was Alan's age, did not stand up.) As soon as the lights came on, the missionary fell on the floor and died. We were all ushered out and went home. But something amazing had happened to Alan and me. God had come into our lives. We could not stop talking about Him! We felt healed and whole inside. We had to tamper it down a little so that my parents would not think something was wrong with us. We supported each other in our future walks of faith. My brother always said to me, "Our Father is God."

Then, after my sophomore year in college, I took a bus ride with my last $35 across the state of Kansas to a summer camp eighteen miles up a Colorado mountain to a work crew at an Inter-Varsity campground. I had been reading about Amy Carmichael's and Hudson Taylor's lives and thought that I needed to find out more about how to be a missionary. (God had spoken to me to be a missionary to China through these biographies.) There, at Bear Trap Ranch, through Bible studies, I met the Person of Jesus Christ who radicalized my life! Not until that summer did I deeply understand that I, the president of our youth groups, and a student with many honors, was a prideful sinner who needed forgiveness. Later I completed a master's degree in American history and taught humanities in several universities. Donald, my husband, had been a pastor for eighteen years and had a seminary degree as well as a master's degree in Christian education. He had also attended Inter-Varsity conferences and met Christ through Bible studies when taking his BS in science at Pepperdine University in California. I was not prepared for the divergent views of Catholics that I met in St. Paul regarding the Word of God. Cavalletti did not emphasize unorthodox theology in Don's class.

The Catholic theology that I was receiving was troublesome to me, but the scriptural lessons were unusually touching and meaningful. I determined to persevere in the class despite definite ostracism by other students, even those I had known before, but who found my questions distasteful. The only people with whom I ate lunch were my husband from the advanced class and the priest. In expressing my concern about the timeline of the Christian church and its conclusion on earth, the priest showed me compassion and cared for me during those three weeks. He said, "Catholics have many interest groups and varieties of ways of looking at Scripture. Please overlook this problem and find the good in the course," which I did. I participated in writing a lesson from Scripture based upon Catechesis guidelines and had an opportunity to present it to half of the class. I heard my traditional words, too many of them, with questions and too much information, and began to see a new way of focusing on one story or concept, rather than many, and how effective that is in spiritual storytelling to children. I determined to become a storyteller in this mode and to allow myself to change to be able to give children the truth and simple beauty of the Word of God.

During the weeks in the course, I was able to attend Donald's class with Sofia as teacher several times and found her kind, charming, inspiring, and a woman of admiration for my husband's Bible study ability and materials. No one in the class had heard about the value of a concordance! After class, Donald and I drove to a nearby Christian bookstore and purchased more than twenty concordances, took them back to his class, and sold them to the Catholics!

Sofia and Donald built a strong relationship as well. She enjoyed and thrived on his questions, and in a few years, accepted us into her villa in Rome to observe a lesson to Italian children by a Catechesis instructor. I saw the youngest children being respectful and joyful in receiving the story of the Good Shepherd in Italian. After the lesson, they were mainly interested in trying on the Catholic child-size priestly garments.

> *"Ten or so children, from perhaps five to eight years, were fully children (chatting and laughing), but yet open and hungry for God. They were eager to talk and yet respectful to their teachers."*

After being welcomed into the parlor and having introductions and snacks, Sofia gave us some true mustard seeds from her window planter and introductions to visit Montessori schools in Rome before we returned home. When we visited two schools, we never saw a Catechesis lesson being given, so we concluded that probably these lessons were primarily being received by children in Sofia's weekly atrium classes at her villa.

Sofia's materials were hand-made, simple, and beautiful. I was inspired to re-create the materials myself and to ask God to anoint me with the ability to see and understand essentiality and to "let go" and trust that the Holy Spirit would teach the children the truth. Sofia allowed me to trace the two-dimensional parable materials and to photograph them and all her materials on the shelves. I was inspired to expand, enrich, complete, and add a full spiritual dimension to our Montessori classrooms. I did not know that I would have the time to re-think the materials, complete their creation, and practice with them from 1984 to 1989 in the US, to show them to our students in Montessori training in Kent, Washington, and then to have the opportunity to teach these lessons for nearly thirty years, from 1989-2018, in Taiwan, South Korea, the Philippines, Sri Lanka, Viet Nam, and China. Then, in 2018, the crackdown on Christians in China, especially for foreigners, became dangerous.

In the late 1980s, following the course, I discovered a carpenter on an island in Puget Sound who could make sets of parable figures from one-quarter inch plywood. He cut, sanded, and prepared the figures to be painted, and I set up an art space in my living room to reproduce Sofia's colorful parable figures. I found an excellent Christian artist who spent a year painting all the figures in four sets. God opened the way for me to find many stores that were selling their nativity materials at the end of the Christmas season, including many small home objects to make two-year-old Jesus' home look real. I was always on the search for these items and was able to set them up in our four classrooms in Kent, Washington. At least one teacher in each classroom, or more, learned how to give lessons, sing a song of faith, allow the children to pray, and pray simply with them. With one shelf of beginning materials in each classroom, for thirty-six years, the children came and went, thriving in telling the stories to each other. The children would even correct each other's way of telling the story. One day I heard two four-year-old girls telling the Lord's Supper Part 2 story to each other, interacting and discussing as they went:

> Girl #1 said to the other, "This bread reminds you of my body, broken for you. Take and eat."
> Girl #2 replied, "No, that's not how it goes! You have to say, 'This bread is my body, broken for you.'" Both girls were confident that their way was the right way!

I continued to watch and listen and heard them agree to disagree and to finish the lesson together. I realized that I had just witnessed the age-old dispute over "transubstantiation."

When we first began giving spiritual lessons to the children in the classrooms, children would often misuse the materials and play with them. We would not correct them in words but would move the figures for them and say the words of the story to get them back on track. It worked! I remember a boy who had the Good Shepherd and sheep on a floor rug. Then he began to move the Good Shepherd, with the sheep following, off his rug onto the carpet, to the other side of the room. I said, "I wonder where the Good Shepherd is going." (My voice did not go up as if it were an interrogation.)

He replied, "I am taking him to see the pink tower." I smiled and stepped back. He carried out his purpose and then took the figures back to his rug with satisfaction.

We knew that it could be demeaning to the Word of God for the children to play-act with the materials without the true meaning of the story being seen, but we determined to limit intervention to only what was essential in the story, with few words and to trust the Holy Spirit to teach the children from it. One interesting overview of the classroom gave me new insight:

> "We did not have young children pretending with the classroom work, for instance, as one poured the corn and another child poured rice, from one pitcher to another, saying, 'You be the momma, and I'll be the daddy!' Instead, the children were using the Child and Faith materials, as we called them, to meet their need for storytelling. The children would go to the Child and Faith materials and give lessons to each other. If they went off the storyline a little, we would ignore it if it were non-essential or simply show them the story again. The need for acting and storytelling, like pretending, is strongly within the young child. The children were somehow more grounded in the spiritual reality than in pretend play and felt satisfied. They seemed confident and trusted themselves (and God) as they used the beautiful work. The adults in the room also must be good observers, ready to assist the children but with as little intervention as possible. Storytelling has always been an integral part of the life of humans. Sadly, most twenty-first-century families let the television become the child's storytelling adventure and forget to tell stories of faith in their family history."

It is hard for some Christians we have met to accept this. One year we flew to Tampa, Florida, to give lessons to a group of teachers from a Presbyterian Sunday school. (We left Seattle in the early morning in the dark and arrived in Tampa in the dark!) After discussing the lessons and showing some lessons the next day, the Sunday school superintendent said, "But you have to give them the plan of salvation in every lesson!"

I said, "It may be hard to let go, but we can trust God to bring the children back each week to teach them the whole gospel. They will love to come to your Sunday school class and learn stories with figures that they can use themselves for storytelling. Then they will grow in confidence and ask you questions."

> "This free concept that lacked human adult control was much too open for the Superintendent's authoritarian spirit. It may be an axiom of adult learning that the more education degrees or traditional experience we have, the harder it is to accept a way of teaching that is free in movement, thought, and creativity and to be able to trust the child to teach himself! Even my Montessori-trained husband, with his three advanced degrees, found it hard to follow Sofia's 'law' of essentiality. His spiritual stories were longer, full of drama, and added more questions than the teachers of younger children. He was very effective with adults and older children but probably could have been more attuned to young children by following Sofia's 'essentiality' more closely."

Many amazing things can be seen as you watch the children work. As I write this book, I have been thinking about what has given me the most satisfaction in my life and what I would like to do in the 1,000-year reign of Jesus. I would like to show children how to learn with their brains, eyes, and hands together using three-dimensional materials and then observe them grow and learn to their full potential.

Some children need to work on large, simple projects, such as scrubbing a chair, a floor, or a table. It seems to bring them coordination and determination. One day a three-year-old was scrubbing a table. He scrubbed the top of the table, the legs, and sides with a small brush and rinsed them with a sponge. When I came back to check, he was on his back, on the floor, under the table scrubbing the underneath surface of the table. Children are hard workers and love to scrub, not to get the table shiny and necessarily clean, as adults do, but because they love the process. The doing is what enthralls them.

Chapter 3
Seeing God's Image in the Children's Work and Independence

In the 1970s, I was the director of three early childhood Montessori classrooms, two in one school and one early childhood classroom, and also of an elementary classroom in another school in Topeka, Kansas. We did not have our Child and Faith shelves yet, but many interesting things happened in those classrooms to show me the nature of the child. I remember a three-year-old boy, Joshua, who came with his mother to my classroom to visit. Quick as lightning, he ran to each side of the classroom to see what he could touch. He was totally in sensory overload, handling whatever he could. Class had already been going for a week, and I thought, *Do I really want to deal with this energetic boy? How can I keep up with him?* But we took him into the class the next day. As I expected, he was everywhere, but within a few days, he would sit and watch me give him a lesson, and, after I returned the work to the shelf, he used it. Amazingly he soon picked up the concept of choosing his own "work," taking it to his table and enjoying using it.

Montessori's concept of "spontaneous concentration" showed itself to us. He soon exploded into concentration and found a beginning and ending in each lesson and joyfully put the work away. He never showed his previous unfocused personality in the classroom again.

It was as if he (Joshua) had been on a desert island with no food, and he finally found a feast! Within two weeks, he had begun to choose well, concentrate and find great happiness in the use of his hands, brain, and eyes all working together. When I opened another new classroom in Seattle more than ten years later, I comforted myself the night before class by remembering the amazing hunger of children "to choose," "to do the work," and of Joshua's prodigious persistence in learning from the hands-on materials.

"We saw that, as soon as he experienced 'spontaneous concentration,' he could never turn back. Through his great delight to find independence of movement and choice of work, he taught himself to concentrate and learn. Because the materials fit his needs, he could persevere in work without interruption. With that focus, he was able to absorb how to relate to others in a kind manner, just as the teachers acted and spoke to him. A whole new world had opened before him! Because he was fulfilling his mind's hunger and inner will in the work, he was not bothered with negative and non-productive activity. The young child's teachers can confidently come to "work and play" with young children, assured to know that children really do want to learn with all their beings. This is their God-given heritage as human beings and their purpose in the early years. Joshua would be fifty-two years old today."

To what could we attribute what was happening when he "worked"? Or as we watched his hands leading his eyes and brain to the next interesting pouring or spooning, as if he had been longing for this his entire life? How does the hand open the mind? He was not perfect and still was three years old, but his peace and determination were amazing. This is what Maria Montessori called "the secret of childhood" in her book.

Language for humans is the key to learning, living, and working in a group. Since the Montessori classroom allows freedom of movement and speech, within limits, the children reveal themselves to the adults through words as well as actions. Entering the classroom at three years, they are allowed to talk quietly with each other as they work, thus greatly advancing their vocabulary and facility in speech. The nomenclature of materials is specific and extensive, giving children mastery in the communication of their thoughts. All materials have a specific name, such as "broad stairs" or "movable alphabet." As we have experienced as Christians, God is good at speaking and leading us in whispers to our spirit. He is the author of language, especially respectful language. When children are communicating their needs, feelings, questions, and problems to us, we can see the image of God within them. One year, a mother brought her three-year-old daughter to us and told us that her daughter was not speaking. A family member had abused her, and she clammed up in her pain. Of course, we accepted her, knowing that there could be no environment that would be more healing and therapeutic than the classroom of children her own age and in the safety of love and respect. (We had a Chinese boy one year who spoke no English but mastered basic communication with other children in two weeks.)

The teachers and I began praying for her healing and her language to return and to explode as it usually does. After a month, from September through December, she began to whisper to other children. No one made a comment about it, and we let her develop naturally, but we were praising God for the small steps of language. She was learning to work and enjoy tasks, as well. We kept praying, of course, and wondered what would happen to her speech during the Christmas break. To our great delight, she returned and began speaking to her friends and then to the teachers. The classroom environment is a therapeutic tool of great wonder and power.

Another year I attended a school picnic for our parents, children, and teachers. I met a new father who had a cowboy hat and boots on. I asked him what changes he had seen in his daughter since she began attending, and he said, "Now she is happy!" When the children can use their hands to do activities, guided by their brain and eyes, they feel joy and success. They are changed.

(One year, I asked a sign company to make this sign: "Montessori Plus School, the Place Where the Hand Opens the Mind!" The sign company owner's wife said to her husband, "Do you really want to make that sign and put it out by the road?" He told me that she thought we were spanking the children!)

> "This experience shows the great difficulty in overcoming culturally negative ideas about children in our society. Most often, even Christians think of the youngest children as being mainly selfish and obstinate. When the children's need to 'construct themselves with their hands' is met, they show us a view of God in a marvelous way. The children can concentrate, enjoy learning, and become peaceful and happy. They unconsciously find purpose in their 'work,' and become self-confident beings, even kind to others."

Most adults, when they see their first child, cannot believe the perfection and beauty of the child. We hear the first cry and know that we will never be the same again. We learn by being with our new baby how he learns and what he needs because he teaches us, but we later forget the extraordinary qualities of the young child in his or her first four years. Every pore of the child is absorbing information about this new world and adapting to it. Where does this great need to learn and know come from? What does the child have within him so that he can realize this "secret"? Is he able to understand God in an undefined way that we cannot?

Over nearly fifty years working with young children, I have concluded that children, having just come from God Himself, show us the wonder and glory of God the Creator as we adults are ready and able to see Him. After choosing a "work," Joshua settled his body into a safe, comfortable space and began to do the task. We can then remember what God said to Adam and Eve: *Go into all of the earth and subdue (work) it, naming (and learning about everything) it.* It is our joy as adults to be able to "multi-task" and give a lesson on the floor or table but also to revel in observation of the concentration and self-confidence that the child can have when he is free and independent! One year I had a four-year-old boy who began class late. After his first day in school, when his mother came to pick him up, he said to her, "Guess what, Mom! We don't play here, we 'work.'" Work is purposeful play; it is enabling and gives power and self-confidence to children.

(One year, I asked my four-year-old granddaughter, Teiya, if she would like to go along on a field trip in the afternoon with me and an older class. She said, "Yes, I want to go, and can Riley go too? He knows how to multi-task." *Her brother was only two years old. She must have thought she was saying that he can follow the guidelines and still be safe.* This is my second granddaughter about whom my son said to me when she was six months old, "Mom, when I look at her, I think that she thinks she is in control of the whole world!")

My first granddaughter, Kirsten, was in our school through age ten, having begun at twenty months old. Donald was her first teacher and her last teacher in our elementary school. We had no toddler program, so she was in our mixed-age class (two and a half to six years). Since her mother was teaching in our other school across the Kent valley, Kirsten came early when the teachers were preparing their classroom. First, she got her rug, then took the *h* phonetic bucket from the shelf, put it on her rug, and took out the small "high chair from the bucket." Then she got the *b* phonetic bucket, put it on her rug, found the "baby" inside, and put it on the highchair. She played a while without interruption and then put it away.

> *"The children in our schools are not allowed to pretend and play with the materials at length but are asked to use the learning materials actively, with purpose, and then return them to their shelf. Here is a good example of the importance of setting aside rules for a special child in the mixed-age classroom.*
> *"It is not hard to do this because every one of the twenty children is free to move and choose and therefore openly shows his differences and similarities to others. He will be understood as such. There is beauty in diversity as well as in the adults' recognition of special needs. (This is just like God.)*
> *"Having lived with adults who pray and speak of God, Kirsten also had a special propensity for spiritual lessons and loved to manipulate and tell the Good Shepherd story at her leisure. 'A young child shall lead them.' Imagine seeing a twenty-month-old toddler moving the sheep to follow after the Good Shepherd! Kirsten is now in her twenties and has been working for World Vision as a research analyst for more than nine years. World Vision is a non-profit organization that provides for the needs of disadvantaged children all around the world."*

I had asked the teachers to take special care of Kirsten on the playground, but otherwise, she had an hour to herself early in the morning while teachers were preparing for class but observing her. It was obvious that Kirsten, as a toddler, was in her strong learning period for using her five senses, and her teachers could see that this time was a pleasure for her. They allowed her special space and guidelines since she had exceptional mastery of herself. One time, when I was on the outside deck, I showed the children how to walk carefully on a balance beam. As I began to walk, I said, "I can do this." I put my hands out to my side for balance.

The child who came next asked me before she stepped

onto the board, "What was that you said?" Our positive words of confidence shape the young child's outlook on life.

Another time two children were arguing at the covered sandbox. One of them came to me and asked, "Mrs. McClurkin, what is infinity?"

I replied, "That is when something never ends."

That child went back to the other child and said, "I told you so! Infinity is when something never ends." At about four years old, they seemed to be discussing how much sand was in the sandbox.

Donald and I went to South Korea and spoke at several universities a few times. Afterward, we went to a famous market, E-T-Won, outside of Seoul, and I bought two sets of colorful children's socks for a matching work for Kirsten's classroom. I put six mixed pairs of socks in a basket on the classroom shelf. I noticed that the children were enjoying matching them. About a month later, a teacher in the classroom came and said to me, "The children's sock-matching basket is almost empty." I checked, and sure enough, it was. There was only one pair left. I decided to watch that classroom the next morning and see what was happening. After our first circle, I saw Kirsten go into that room, walk over to the basket on the shelf, take the last pair, and sit on the floor. She removed her slippers, then her own socks, and put on the last pair of matching socks to her own feet. They just fit.

> *"She had found what socks really are for: putting on your own feet, not laying them on a table and matching them! No one else, only the toddler, had found the true use for those special socks. Children are simple and practical. God is like this for us."*

As we use the Child and Faith materials with the children, we silently pray that God will lead them to faith and bring them to His purpose for them in life. We wonder what will happen when they face the inevitable challenges of family and life as they grow up. Will they have internalized the faith lessons that they are learning at our school? How long will they still have this special quality of openness to God?

One day I was driving my big van to the store with Kirsten in the back seat. She was four years old. We were talking, and she asked, "Grandma, are you and Grandpa ever going to have any more babies?" (I was fifty-eight, and Donald was sixty-five.)

I replied, "Kirsten, I don't have any more eggs."

Kirsten said, "Well, Grandma! You know what the Bible says, 'With God nothing is impossible!'"

> *Children easily believe God and what He says. This is what Jesus meant when He said, "Let the little children come to me. Never stop them. For of such is the kingdom of heaven." Later, when Kirsten was about eight years old and a student in our Montessori elementary classroom, at home, she declared to her mother, "When I grow up, I want to go to a Montessori college."*

I thank God that He chose an Italian woman to become a doctor and teacher in the twentieth century. What would education have been like in today's technological age without Maria's understanding of the needs and nature of the young child? If there were no classrooms with freedom of choice, independence, with knowledge encapsulated into manipulative materials, kindness, respect for everyone, non-competition, self-confidence, and trust in the child's ability to teach him or herself? Dr. Maria Montessori is God's gift to humanity to keep us grounded in remembering what the human being really is and what he can become.

Two young boys were wrestling on the playground and began to fight. Donald stepped between them and said, "Let's sit over here and talk." He led the two children to sit on the edge of the deck and said, "When you hit each other, I am worried that you will get hurt. I need everyone to be safe." Boy #1 began to claim loudly that Boy #2 had pushed him.

Boy #2 cried out, "But he pushed me first."

They began yelling and could have begun the fistfight again. But then Donald said, "Please sit here beside each other a while and talk about it. See if you can figure out a way to be friends again."

Donald moved away but not too far and saw the boys talking. After a few minutes, Boy #1 said to the other, "Okay. Can you come to my birthday party?"

Boy #2 said, "Yes, and you can come to *my* birthday party, too!" Donald saw them get up and go out to play together again.

This scenario between young children occurs frequently and is often reconciled without the adult's suggestions. Sometimes the adult will ask the children to pray with him or suggest a solution to which the children will agree. When the conflict is resolved, young children act as if no affront ever happened. They forgive, usually without the adult giving them words of forgiveness, such as "I am sorry that I pushed you." The child often thinks of the ultimate statement of forgiveness, which is, "Will you come to my birthday party?"

> *"I have never heard children who were fighting one day and resolved the problem, only to bring the argument up another day. Forgiveness is forever, just like God's forgiveness."*

In our school, we never ask a child to say, "I am sorry." Instead, the teacher says it for the child to the one who is hurt. "I am sorry that you are hurt." The teacher can say these words in authenticity. When the child is made to say, "I am sorry," to the other child, he is just parroting the words and probably is not feeling sorry at all. The example of a child asked to sit down in church, who sits down but says, "I may be sitting down on the outside, but I am standing up on the inside," is surely true. The teacher usually really feels sorry about the hurt. She is the model and mentor for the child.

> *"If a child continues to be aggressive and out-of-control many times, the other children will usually avoid that child or keep a distance, and wait until the child learns how to act, to be sure that there is not another confrontation. This is self-protection."*

When children come to our school and begin to be free, we wonder how the concepts of freedom of choice, self-confidence, kindness, and forgiveness will be accepted by their parents. Most parents have not thought about their child's ability to learn these concepts at an early age. Our school is a community. (The children notice when someone is missing.) Here are a few examples of unwitting parental interference in their child's growth:

1. A set of older parents pulled up to the school in their truck, with their four-year-old child in the middle of the front seat. They brought him in, and I saw him hesitate to stay the longer they were there. Finally, they left, and we greeted him and invited him to work. I showed him a simple work, but after I put it away, he did not take it. He wandered and watched, which is normal for the first day. He was fours year old, which means that he missed his three-year-old year when he could have been more spontaneous in relation to the lessons. As the week went on, and then two weeks, we did not see him engaging in any lessons. I began to be concerned and observed him daily. Finally, I realized that he was afraid to choose work. He had to be given "a lesson" on how to choose work, whereas the three-year-old usually engages and can choose and do work automatically. (We guessed that his parents must have been closely controlling him.) The next

day at the beginning of work time, I invited him to the art shelf. We chose a work together (it was his choice), and I showed him how to cut on the lines. I returned the work to the shelf, stayed near him, and said, "Now you may do it." He took the work and did it. I realized that he needed to have permission to take the work, touch it, and use it, probably due to his parents' choosing most things in his life: food, clothing, activities, etc., when he was born to choose.

One of the noblest parts of being a human is the right and opportunity to choose, which obviously comes to us from the nature of God. A child who is not allowed to choose is missing this huge part of their heritage. To help adults remember this, we try to follow this guideline, "Whatever a child can do for himself, he should be allowed to do." The boy began to use work with great interest.

2. When I was greeting the children in the hall one year, four-year-old Molly's mother brought her and came into the hallway. (Parents were asked to leave their child at the door.) Her mother pulled off Molly's coat and hung it up for her. For several days the same scenario happened. I would say, "Molly can do this herself," but her mother did not answer. Since Donald was Molly's teacher, I told him about this. The next day, Donald was in the hallway, and Molly's mother began to take off Molly's coat. Donald said to Molly, "Molly, please show your mother how you can hang up your own coat!" Her mother replied for Molly, "I know that she can do it for herself, but I like to do it!"

> *Molly's mother's own desires were more important to her than Molly's growth of confidence and independence. Sometimes parents want to keep their children from growing up too quickly!*

3. A teacher in our school was having marital problems, especially with being hit by her husband. When talking with her, I discussed the fact that we do not spank children at school. She was surprised and said, "But the Bible says, 'Spare the rod and spoil the child.'"

   I answered, "This scripture can be understood as a rod of leadership, not pain. David said in Psalm 23, 'Thy rod and thy staff, they comfort me.' The shepherd does not beat His sheep with His rod but directs and protects him with it."

She left with her son to go to their car, and from the office window I was shocked to see that he was wildly hitting her with both arms and hands. He did not want to go home, but she gathered him up and put him into the car. I meditated on this scene to understand it. Why was he so angry? I think that he learned from both his mother and his father that hitting back in anger was the way to protect himself.

> *His mother was also probably overly controlling as well, and he did not want to leave the school where he was free to choose and free not to be hit.*

4. Our assistant teachers are interns for a year in our school. They learn and follow the school guidelines, such as the fact that children wear water aprons when they do water work. The teachers follow the same rules. One year, a girl, about four, was receiving a lesson on using a baster from an intern,

but he had forgotten to put on his apron. Melissa looked at him and said, "Mr. Kenny, you need your apron!" But the intern kept going. She said again, "You need your apron!" Mr. Kenny did not stop. Then Melissa said, "Mr. Kenny, if you keep going like that, you will never become a teacher!"

> *She had the self-confidence to speak the truth to him and believed that teachers and adults "go by" the same rules! This is God's view of humankind: equality.*

5. A father came to the door of my classroom and asked to speak with me. My class was small, so I went to the door. He said, "I am going to withdraw my daughter (age three and a half) from your school. Since she has been coming here, she will not obey me immediately." (He was in a military uniform.)
   I replied, "You're worried!"
   "Yes," he said. "I ask her to do something, and she answers, 'Why?'"
   There was nothing that I could say to change his mind, but I thought, *With your being such a strict father, just wait until she is a teenager!*

> *It is better to respond now and grow gradually with her in answering her questions about independence than to wait for her teenage years! It may be too late then.*

6. In one of our schools, one-third of our parents were psychiatrists. A family of husband and wife psychiatrists brought their three- and four-year-old boys to our school. Their mother usually brought them and left them at the outside gate with a teacher,

saying to them, "Work hard, boys!" The boys, however, would not choose any work that showed them a beginning, middle, and end. They would only cut line paper all day. In one day, they could consume all of the paper-cutting materials, so I brought out recycled newspapers for them to cut. (In our classrooms, we try to "follow the child" as long as it is helpful to them.) They cut up all of the newspapers.

After about a week, I asked their mother at the gate what the boys did on weekends. She said that they had special lessons all day, such as personal defense, horseback riding, Chinese language lessons, etc. Then I asked, "Do they have time to play, relax, and have fun together?"

She answered, "Well, Mrs. McClurkin, after all, we are preparing them for Harvard!"

I thought, *If you only knew what they are really doing in the classroom... They may be wasting your money and their time here.*

The next day I asked the boys, "Why are you so busy cutting paper?"

They replied, "We are 'making money.'" That afternoon I removed all of the scissors from the classroom and watched what would happen. The boys looked for scissors and could not find them, so they looked around for other "work" and began to engage in all of the materials. They showed a normal and noble interest in hands-on learning.

> *For the good of even one child, all of the children can make a small, temporary sacrifice, unknown to them and the other children, that will impact the quality of learning for all of the classroom.*

7. A beautiful banker's wife, in stylish clothing, brought her handsome three-year-old son to our school. He stayed beside her as long as he could,

then I took him into the classroom. We showed him several lessons, but he would not engage nor respond to our invitation, "Now it is your turn." After a few weeks of observing the classroom and others, most children find the natural urge and courage within themselves to learn and explore, but not Eric.

We were pleased when his mother invited the three female teachers to lunch at their mansion. We hoped that we would gain some clues as to Eric's inability to choose. (Donald and I always gave an invitation to each parent to invite us to their home, if they would like, to get to know each other.)

It was a lovely lunch, without Eric at the table, and the first time that I had ever had "quiche lorraine." After lunch, his mother asked, "Would you like to see Eric's playroom?" We followed her to the basement and discovered that the entire periphery was filled with shelves of playschool toys. It could have been a playschool store. We thought, *No wonder Eric will not touch the learning materials at school! It's like his "touching mechanism" has been worn out. His brain and hands can't take in anything more.* With sensitive and careful diligence, we continued to invite him to simple work, and finally, he took off. It took about a month for him to come to his "work."

Dr. Montessori discussed the problem of poor children who come to the classroom and do not have a spontaneous response to the materials of learning, but it is also true for the wealthy child. At least his mother had purchased shelves and placed the toys in some order. The image of God within the children can be distorted until gentle invitations to work can be made.

A child who was living in a car showed the same response to the learning materials. She was also hesitant to touch and unsure of her right to do so.

Chapter 4
The Child's Freedom to Learn Releases the Image of God within Him: Making Good Choices, Self-Confidence, Kindness, Forgiveness, and More

Because young children often drop things, it is common for the entire class to hear a "thud" of something falling to the floor. The whole classroom stops and becomes silent. Then many of the children stop their work and go to help the child who spilled something. (Not if it is glass.) No one asks them to do it, but they take this upon themselves as a "family-classroom." No child blames the child. It is as if they all realize that it could happen to them. They keep on helping until it is all back in place. Most adults in our culture believe that young children are competitive and selfish, but I know that in their young years they show amazing kindness to each other. I believe that this helpful and kind spirit is within the child naturally, in the image of God, and is encouraged by the Montessori concept of non-competition. The theory is that we all try to do our best and even help others when needed. This is a relaxing, stress-free environment and sets the pace for all the learning. God does not have nor need to have a competitive spirit.

Amazingly, children are experiencing real freedom in body, mind, and heart, and they assume responsibility beyond their years. They truly believe that they can do anything! Once my son-in-law said to his four-year-old daughter, Kirsten, "you act like you can do anything!"

She answered, "I can!"

I remember a three-year-old girl crying and crying after her mother left her at school. Finally, another girl, who just a few days before was crying when her mother left her, went over to her and said, "Don't cry! Your mother will be back." Then she returned to her work. I was able to see this scenario again the following year when a child was crying hard, and the girl who was crying the year before went up to this year's crying child and said, "Don't worry! Your mother will be back." The empathy for hurting children is palpable.

In my first years of Montessori education, I struggled with the concept of non-competition. Maybe no child could have been more competitive than I: I was the oldest child in the family and a girl with three brothers. In the car and on the farm, my brother, Alan, and I made up games and stories with the help of our grandfather. After being in the "guinea pig" (gifted) class during junior high school, I expected to be treated equally with boys. In my sophomore high school geometry class, however, my old geometry teacher began the school year by stating that she had never given an A to a girl!

I was the wrong girl to say that to. I had become one of the top learners of the thirty children in the gifted class. I studied constantly; I read Anson's biology and chemistry college textbooks. I made it a policy to ask myself, "What else can I do better for tomorrow's assignment?" I did all the extra credit homework that was offered, often thinking about my gifted father, who was pre-med and also a teaching assistant. (My aunt had told me stories about his intelligence and that he had a photographic memory, was a poet, and musician.) I told my brother, Alan, all about him, behind closed doors. I was determined to complete my father's MD degree and to become the doctor he could not become. (After I was introduced to humanities in my junior year of college, however, I changed my major to biological studies with a history minor. I became infatuated with a search to find God's image in the beauty of his gifts of human creativity through the centuries: music, literature, art, science, philosophy, government, and religion.)

I got an idea: I asked my friend, Jo, who had been in the gifted class with me if she could get me one of the geometry books that her teacher was using in her class across the hall. I got it and studied it as well as every "extra credit" question at the end of each chapter. I was fifteen. When I answered a question in my class that no one else could answer, the boy in front of me turned around and said, "You're good at this, aren't you?" When we got our grades at the end of the year, the teacher gave me an A-. In those days, we did not question our teacher's grading, but I knew she wanted to keep saying that no girl had ever gotten an A in her class.

Eventually, I was able to reconcile my competitive spirit with my classroom's basic philosophy by working with young children and watching them thrive when no one was comparing them with another child. (I had been number 499 out of 500 in my high school graduation class. My parents never knew. My name was at the top of the graduation program, but they never mentioned that they saw it.) In January 1959, I began a venture of faith and applied for a three-year National Defense Education Act PhD Fellowship in humanities from Florida State University. I stood on Romans 4:20 and every day believed God would take me to graduate school. In May, I was in my Greek class when I received a telegram awarding me a full three-year $6,600 fellowship, the largest ever granted to a student at my Christian college. I married Donald after one year of MA studies in American history.

In my first year of Montessori teaching, after my "internship" year, I tried many ways to help children think and act with creativity in the classroom: bringing a lamb into the hallway before circle, a python and a tarantula in cages, and a guinea pig in the hall (until he died from overeating carrots and vegetables the children brought him.) The children enjoyed running on the playground with a large lop-eared rabbit on a collar and rope. Someone stole that rabbit from the cage from our playground on Easter eve.

In the summer, we enjoyed the "open door policy" of children having the freedom to move inside and outside at their wish, with a teacher coming along with them. (The back and front gates were locked in for safety.)

> *"We discovered that, for the first few days of freedom, the children loved to stay outside. After a while, however, most of the children preferred to come inside and work with the materials. When I recorded the times, I found that the time inside the classroom and outside eventually evened out to about the same as our prescribed schedule of two hours of work time and one-half hour outside. This was also true of field trip days: as soon as the children returned to the school, they wanted to come inside and work, not play on the playground. Their inner need for work had not been satisfied."*
> *"Without hands-on work during the day, the children did not want to go home."*

The four-year-old children began to read. One afternoon I found a four-year-old boy reading a full book to three children who had climbed onto empty wall shelves in a corner and were lying on the shelves, listening intently to him.

With a two-story school building, I tried an experiment. I arranged the classrooms with one academic area on each floor (language or math), but the other complete areas were divided between two floors. Children had "freedom within limits" to move between two floors. To my surprise, the children who could not concentrate mainly enjoyed running up and down the back stairway and avoided consequences of misbehavior from teachers by fleeing to the other floor. Not surprisingly, the teachers could not keep track of the work done by any of the forty-eight children who were in the two classrooms that month!

> "In the 90s, I saw a variation of this model in South Korea, but the children moved to different classrooms on certain days of the week. That was not a healthy model, either. This was an arrangement by the power of the adult, not the choice of the children. Children need a constant, limited, predictable learning environment to give them a foundation of stability. God knows our human need for order and adult supervision and provides us with parents to care for their children."

But I read and admired Montessori's work and found that she had more than twenty-four children at her "circle times," ages two and a half to six years, and used snack time at circle as an introduction to "grace and courtesy." So did I for my twenty-four children.

When we played "Walking Music," the twenty-four mixed-age children gathered and walked on the circle line until the teacher sang, "Please sit down." Then I brought a tray of snacks (apple slices and Graham crackers), a paper bowl, and a napkin holder with twenty-four napkins. As the children all sat with their legs crossed. I called each child's name to come to get their snack: "Beth, would you care for a snack? Please say, 'Yes, please,' or 'No, thank you.'" Then the child comes to get the snack, takes the paper bowl, chooses a piece of apple and a cracker, and puts them into the bowl, takes a napkin, then says thank you, and the teacher answers, "You are welcome." The teacher then says, "Please wait to eat until everyone is served." After everyone is served, then the teacher will thank God for the food, and we would eat. Sometimes you may have a child in the class who loves to pray aloud. Once, I had a child who raised her hand and asked if she could sing a "solo" at the circle. She did, although very much off-key!

After a few days of this, when half of the children were served but not yet eating, "Bobby," a four-year-old boy raised his hand and asked, "Mrs. McClurkin, did Dr. Montessori make all of the children wait to eat until everyone was served?"

I replied, "Bobby, I don't know the answer to that, but I will try to look it up. Thank you for your question." I did not find an answer, but the next day I began thanking God for the snack before anyone came to take it, and then said, "Please eat your snack after you take it, and place your paper cup and napkin into the center trash can."

> *"How did a four-year-old boy have the courage (no fear) and feel comfortable to ask his teacher such a cogent question? Rather than complaining, he sought to solve the problem, and he did. Bobby's humble but self-confident question showed unusual perception but also a deep assurance that only comes through work. He wanted a fair and equitable service of snack to his friends, young and a little older. He trusted me to be kind to him. Eventually, we allowed the children to take and eat their snacks at the four-person table at the time of their choice during work time."*

Chapter 5
The Need and Love for Reality Come from God's Image within Children

One year I decided to experiment with the children's understanding of reality. I told them the Greek fable about a farmer and his son who took a donkey to market. The fable goes like this:

> Once there was a farmer who wanted to take his donkey to market. He asked his son to go with him, and the two held the donkey's rope and walked down the road. When they came to a village, someone said to them, "How silly of you! You should be riding the donkey, rather than leading it!" So, the son got on the donkey, and they continued to market. However, soon after they passed by, some other people said, "How cruel you are! You are a young man. Your father should be riding on the donkey!" Then both the father and son got on the donkey. They continued down the road and passed through another village. People in the village cried out,

"You are too heavy to be riding the donkey! You should be carrying him yourself!" So, the father and son tied the donkey's legs to a big stick and began carrying the donkey over their shoulders to market. Just as they passed over a bridge, the donkey struggled to get free and fell into the river and drowned. I asked the children, "What is this story all about? What should the farmer do?"

A four-year-old boy, Sean, raised his hand and answered, "The father should jump into the river and save the donkey!"

> *"Of course, the story is about following your own good judgment, rather than others', but the pragmatic answer for a child had to be about the fate of the donkey. That is what concerned a child."*

Experiments have been done with young children with two-sided, colored paper. If you fold the paper in half and ask a two or three-year-old child what color the paper is, whichever color they can see will be the color they name for the paper. They insist that is the color. It does not matter if you explain to them that the paper is another color on the other side. "Seeing is believing!" A cup of water is whatever color of food coloring that you put into it, even though the child watches you put in the coloring. It could no longer possibly be just the color of water.

Another year a teacher brought her black scuba outfit to class and showed and carefully held up each part of the outfit and named it. Then she told the children that she was going into the bathroom to put it all on to show them and did so. We sang a few songs while we waited for her to return and when she came out of the bathroom with flippers, helmet, and all covered in black, the children saw her and screamed and ran from the circle. One child said, "It's a monster!" Even though she gave the children knowledge of each piece of the scuba outfit, nevertheless, no words could console the children of their fears of a black monster. When she took off the helmet in front of them and then put it back on in front of them, they still screamed and called her a monster. Reality for children is what they see with their own eyes.

For George Washington's birthday, I brought in a book about what he ate for breakfast, *George Washington's Breakfast*. We read a few pages every day and saw a few things about his life. I borrowed my brother's size 12 boots and put them on the piano bench and said, "This is the size of George Washington's boots." All week long, the children walked by those boots and said to each other, "Those are George Washington's boots!" Then I brought in a real horseshoe and told them the myth that many people at the time he lived said that he was so strong that he could straighten a horseshoe.

When I asked them if they thought he could do that, they said, "Yes," but when I passed around the horseshoe, and they tried to straighten it themselves, they tried to do so, felt the metal, and tried and said, "No."

That week each child made their own three-sided hat. On Friday, we finished the book that told the story that George Washington made pancakes for breakfast on a hoe on a fire out on the field. We prepared the batter; the children poured their own pancake batter into an electric skillet and flipped the pancake under teacher supervision. Four of the children sat together at a table, eating their pancakes and wearing their three-sided hats, and one child said, "I really feel like George Washington!"

One Friday, I told the children that next week we would find out what sound *j* makes and that I would play a little joke on them. While they were leaving their morning work the next Monday and coming to circle, I went into the bathroom and put on a long dress, a white wig, black lines on my face, white gloves, came out to circle with a cane and said, in a wobbly voice, "Good morning, children! I am Mrs. McClurkin's grandmother!" The room became perfectly silent.

After a minute, one four-year-old boy said loudly, "I know who you really are! You are Mrs. McClurkin. I see the freckles on your arms." Everyone laughed, and I took off my wig, and they laughed more.

I said, "This is my joke. *Joke* begins with the sound of *j*." For weeks afterward, the children would come up to me and say, "I remember when your grandmother came to circle!" Even the following year, some children reminded me of it. Some of them really thought that my grandmother had come to school.

I met a mother who told me that rather than enrolling her son in our school, she was going to spend her son's three to five years going to museums, beaches, train rides, and everywhere she could to explore the world with him. I thought that sounded like fun, but it was wrong. Young children, of course, need to see what the world is and what is in it, but even more, they need to be able to touch, see up close, hear and taste and smell on their own, and make it work. This is the sensitive period for using all the senses oneself and actually causing the environment to work to teach yourself. Then the child experiences power, and experimentation, and the world himself. Let us be very careful to balance cartoon figures and human replicas with reality when working with children so that they can figure out what is real. The parable figures are two-sided replicas of humans who lived during Jesus' life, but the figures of humans who really lived are three-dimensional and lifelike.

It is interesting to know that experiments have been done to show that the child's mind can view miniatures and envision them as life-like. If you show a child a dollhouse, and then hide a small doll under a bed, then hide a full-size doll under a similar-looking full-size bed in a similar real bedroom, the child can find it. We humans can imagine and compare and find similarities and differences in the world, especially if we begin when we are children. Children are learning every day about reality and how to deal with it. Once I was in a two-year-old's living room of my adult student. The son popped a VHS cassette into the player, pushed a button, and on came *Dumbo the Elephant*. He and I watched for a while, and then I asked him, "Michael, do you think that elephants really can fly?"

He replied, "Yes." The antidote to this misunderstanding of reality, of course, is to take the child to the zoo. When he sees the huge elephant body and thick legs, he will see the truth.

In my early years as a mother, I taught history of Western civilization for a few years, then took ten years off to be a full-time mother of three children and pastor's wife, followed by owning and directing Montessori schools and teaching children for twenty years. I was also a Montessori trainer for forty-three years. With my BS in biological sciences and an MA in history, I enjoyed observing children, telling their stories, and "wondering" about their nature and relationships with God.

Occasionally I would "find" myself in the child that I was working with. Dr. Montessori called this "recapitulation": I saw a little girl with red braids and a top knot, and so many freckles that that was all you could see on her face, working in the classroom. I heard a little girl asking so many questions that, finally, when she asked her uncle, who was ten years older, what something was for, he answered, "To make little girls like you ask questions!"

Chapter 6
The Teacher as Observer of God's Image and Mentor of Respect

This book is a partial autobiography of Sharlet McClurkin, but it is also about Maria Montessori's educational theory, biblical theology, and twenty-five prototype lessons on Spiritual Storytelling using Sofia Cavalletti's model. Here are two experiences that I have had in the last three years:

I read an article in a Christian magazine about the success of a church that was sending teachers to a nearby public elementary school for Release Time. I remembered when my husband's church in St. Paul, Minnesota, had participated successfully in Release Time, which is usually one hour per week when children may stay at school for special activities given by local churches. The teachers use this time for meetings and preparation. Children whose parents are home may leave, and the rest of the children stay at school and receive Bible stories, craft experiences, and outdoor play. I began praying that God would open the door of the local public elementary school for our church to have an opportunity to do this. Not long afterward, the pastor announced that our closest elementary school had invited our church to participate in Release Time, and he invited the congregation to volunteer. I did and explained that I had special lessons on the life and parables of Jesus to show to the children. My friend, the assistant pastor, accepted me. I agreed to teach for six weeks.

I was eighty years old. I prepared a rolling cart with the Good Shepherd lesson and a cloth for surprise. I lifted the cart into the back seat of my Prius and arrived at the elementary school at about three p.m. I then pulled the cart into the school from the parking lot, went into the school, signed in, and found the meeting room. Already, about half a dozen volunteers from the church were there. I found a low table, put out the Good Shepherd lesson, and covered it with a cloth. A few children were already there and intrigued but did not touch the "work." About fifteen loud, lively ten-year-old children ran into the room. The adult in charge asked them to sit on the rug on the floor and to turn toward my lesson. I had been told that I would have fifteen to twenty minutes to teach.

The adult introduced me, and I said, "I have grandchildren your age; I want to tell you a story." Most of the children listened and scooted closer. I told them a very few things about myself, and then I said that when I was their age, my father was shot in Italy in a war by a German tank. Everything exploded! One boy asked, "What kind of tank was it?"

Another boy asked, "Did he die?"

I said, "Yes," and they kept asking questions. Shortly, I said, "Well, the story I have to tell you is not about a tank, but about a Shepherd and His sheep. I have forgiven the Germans for killing my father."

I realized that I had breached Cavalletti's rule of "essentiality," but I began the story and moved the Good Shepherd to the sheepfold and placed the ten sheep inside, and then to the pasture. Suddenly the anointing of God came upon us all. The children began asking rapid-fire questions about God, and I answered them. They did not want to stop talking. I gave the whole lesson and then sang, "Amazing Grace." I prayed with them to know God and left. The teachers took the children into another room to work on crafts. Afterward, the assistant pastor said that he had never seen anything like that before. The children were amazing!

I gave five more lessons, which the children listened to, but there was no special anointing on them. More adults came to visit, however, and watched the lessons. One teacher asked me if my lessons were online. Then, Release Time ended for the school year. In other weeks and at church, several people expressed interest in the lessons, and one woman called me the "story-telling lady," but no one ever mentioned a word about Release Time next year. My pastor friend thanked me, but I waited for them to speak to me about next year. A year later, on Sunday, the pastor again invited volunteers for Release Time from the pulpit, but no one spoke to me about teaching or not. No one explained to me that I would not be teaching, but a friend said to me that she had heard that the church had purchased a printed curriculum for Release Time and would be using it. For several weeks I waited for further information and never heard any. For several months I felt sad and wondered why they had left me out. I felt old and unimportant, but soon I was able to forgive and forget and go on with my summer training class in China. I had had an experience with fifteen to twenty older children, whom I believed had learned much, as had I!

What I learned about teaching Child and Faith lessons from that experience was that storytelling with figures is very effective with older children, but adults perhaps find it too simple and somewhat unorthodox.

Two years ago, a teacher of about thirty-five years of age came to the US from an African country on our school's student visa. My husband had passed away two years before he came. Ibrahim lived in my spare bedroom and cooked his food in my kitchen. We shopped together and made an unlikely pair. He became like a son. But he worked hard and received his teaching certificate, returning home to begin a Montessori school for about fifty children. I had given him several Child and Faith lesson materials, such as the Good Shepherd, and he faithfully showed them to his children in his own classroom. He has also trained assistants to give Montessori lessons. Now he and I are helping a second camp of refugees find work and meaning in their lives. He is teaching two young men to ride his motorcycle ten miles away to that second camp and to show forty children the Good Shepherd lesson and other faith lessons. One morning, Ibrahim arranged for someone to bring twenty young children to the Montessori classroom from the second camp ten miles away. They stayed for the morning, and the twenty-five young members of that current class found a partner and showed the new children how to use the learning materials. Afterward, someone asked the new children, "When will you be back?"

And they said, "Tomorrow!"

It is my dream that many teachers will find the Child and Faith lessons inspiring and meaningful for young children. These lessons from the Scriptures will change the classroom and the teacher who can learn to observe the image of God within the young children and their work. Even though the children will succumb to the natural laws of maturation in our society, they will never forget the foundation from God that they received in these early years. These young children are the hope of the world! They are not empty, waiting for the teacher to fill them, but they are full of God's nature and His image. In private early childhood classrooms and home schools, atriums (open classrooms) can be set up all over the US. Teachers can find inspiration, hope, and joy as they "work" and "play" and "learn" with the children: more about how children learn and how God teaches them. My email is childandfaith@gmail.com.

Part 2

Storytelling from the Life and Parables of Jesus Principles of Best Practices of Biblical Storytelling

Basic Principle: Young children (and seniors) learn best through hearing stories and watching figures move to the narratives from God's Word.

- Allowing children (and seniors) to "wonder" about God's Word gives the Holy Spirit an opportunity to teach these special groups of people.
- Leading a short prayer and singing a related song of worship seals the multi-sensory experience from God's Word. The participants go home, theologizing in their own way!
- No more than one lesson will be shown in one hour or one-half day so as to allow the singular purpose of the lesson to be understood and felt. All twelve materials will be available to view and photograph.
- The best lifelike figures for the five infancy narratives can be purchased online from Fontanini's company. They are more than $10 per figure but are made of strong materials and excellent color and artwork.

Would you like to learn how to present a fifteen to twenty-five-minute story about Jesus that focuses on one spiritual concept in a multi-sensory experience? Sunday school children, early release children, and seniors in rest homes and care centers are hungry for a faith concept that is easy to understand and meets their innermost needs.

Learn how to make God's Son a personal reality to those who are young, discouraged, or tired and hurting.

Find out how to create an atmosphere of joy and wonderment toward God!

Feel the joy of allowing children (and others who are in a place of spiritual openness to God) to ask questions, deep or superficial, and receive meaningful answers.

These twelve lessons will whet your desire to study the Word of God and to write and give your own storytelling lessons to those around you: The Good Shepherd; The Visit of the Wise Kings; The Found Sheep; The Found Son; The Announcement to Mary; The Pearl of Great Price; The Announcement of the Shepherds; Lifetimes (Resurrection); The Birth of Jesus; The Lord's Supper; The Ten Secrets of a Happy Life; and The Door. These are twelve of the twenty-five lessons that we have created and have told young children for more than thirty-five years.

The Good Shepherd

The Good Friend

The Found Sheep

The Found Coin

The Found Son

The Ten Maidens

The Parable of Prayer

The Four Soils

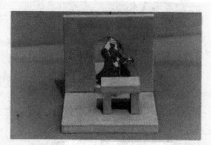

The Pearl of Great Price

The Wedding Garment

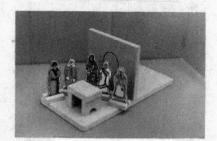

The Lord's Supper, Part 3

Index: Suggested Sequence of Materials for Young Children

(In Order of Difficulty)

1. The Good Shepherd
   John 10:1-14
   "In God's Green Pastures Feeding;" "The Lord Is My Shepherd"

2. The Found Sheep
   Luke 15:4-7
   "Amazing Grace"

3. The Announcement to Mary
   Luke 1:26-38
   "I Love You, Lord"

4. The Announcement to the Shepherds
   Luke 2:8-15
   "Praise the Name of Jesus"

5. The Birth of Jesus
   Luke 2:1-7
   "Jesus Christ is Born Today"

6. The Visit of the Shepherds
   Luke 2:8-14
   "Go, Tell It on the Mountains"

7. The Visit of the Wise Kings
   Matthew 2:1-12
   "O Worship the King"

8. The Pearl of Great Price
   Matthew 13:45-46
   "Lord, You Are More Precious Than Silver"

9. The Found Son
   Luke 15:11-24
   "Your Lovingkindness is Greater Than Life"

10. The Resurrection (The Forever Life)
    John 11:25
    "I Am the Resurrection and the Life"

11. The Found Coin
    Luke 15:8-10
    "I Will Enter His Gates with Thanksgiving in My Heart"

12. Creation
    Genesis 1:1-3
    "He's Got the Whole World In His Hands"

13. The Ten Secrets to a Happy Life
    Portions of Exodus 20
    "Thy Word is a Lamp unto My Feet;" "How I Love Thy Law, O Lord"

14. The Good Friend
    Luke 10:30-36

"O I Love You with the Love of the Lord"

15. The Parable of Prayer
Luke 11:5-10
"Seek You First the Kingdom of God"

16. The Four Soils
Matthew 13:3-9
"Father, I Adore You"

17. The Mustard Seed
Matthew 13:31-32
"Jesus, Name Above All Names"

18. The Leaven
Matthew 13:33
"O Magnify the Lord"

19. The Lord's Supper, Part 1
Matthew 26:26-28
"Glorify Thy Name"

20. The Lord's Supper, Part 2
Matthew 26:26-28
"Jesus, What a Wonder You Are"

21. The Lord's Supper, Part 3
Matthew 26:26-28
"We Are One in the Spirit, We Are One in the Lord"

22. The Ten Young Maidens
Matthew 25:1-13
"Worthy, Worthy, Worthy is the Lamb"

23. The Wedding Garment
Matthew 22:1-14
"I Worship You, Almighty God"

24. The Door
    Revelation 3:20
    "Amazing Grace"

25. The Great Commandment
    Mark 12:2-8
    "How I Love Thy Law, O Lord!"

Spiritual Storytelling for Young Children: Child and Faith Lessons (Name the Children Use)

Lesson 1
The Good Shepherd

Materials:
Wooden tray; two-dimensional basket; colored wooden figures on small stands (Good Shepherd figure, ten sheep, wooden circular sheepfold on green wooden circle with outer fence, and second green circle for pasture); and silk cloth to cover everything. (Note: A picture will be placed at the side of each lesson.)

Paraphrased Reading of Scripture from Pocket Bible:
"I have a special story to tell you. It is from the Word of God." Read portions of John 10:1-14 (only those portions that are in the foundation narrative).

Age:
Two and a half to six years and up.

Direct Purpose:
To tell the children about the wonderful love and mercy of God.

Presentation:
Many years ago, a wonderful person lived on this earth. He said many amazing things. There had never been anyone like Him before.

1. Tell the children, "One day someone asked this special person, 'Who are you?' He said, '*I am the Good Shepherd.*'" Uncover the basket, take the Good Shepherd figure out of it, and stand Him inside the sheepfold near its door.

   "He says, 'I have many sheep whom I love very much. This is my sheepfold where the sheep can sleep at night.' Bring out each of the ten sheep figures, one by one, from the basket and stand them in the sheepfold. He says, 'I am the gate. I protect my sheep in the sheepfold where they will be safe at night.'" Lay down the sheep on their sides in the fold. Say, "The Good Shepherd says, 'I am the door of the sheepfold. No one can come in and out except by me.'" Then lay down the Good Shepherd in front of the door, inside the sheepfold.

2. Then stand up the Good Shepherd just inside the door. He says, "In the morning, I call my sheep by

name, each one, saying, 'Come to the pasture, to the green grass and quiet water that I have prepared for you. Come!'" Move the sheep, one by one, to follow closely behind the Good Shepherd to the pasture.

3. You say, "As He walks to the pasture, the Good Shepherd says, 'When I call them, the sheep come, because they know my voice. They follow me, not the voice of a stranger. They know I will lead and protect them. I will give them every good thing. I love my sheep so much, and they love me. I am their Good Shepherd.'" Continue to move the sheep to the pasture. They face Him but spread out to begin to eat the green grass.

4. You say, "The Good Shepherd speaks to them and says, 'I have come to give you a full life of peace and joy. I know you, each one. I will never leave you nor forsake you. I would even lay down my life for you. I am your Good Shepherd.'" You say, "When the end of the day has come, the Good Shepherd says, 'Come, follow Me. We must go back to the sheepfold. Follow closely behind Me and listen for My voice.'" The Good Shepherd moves carefully to the sheepfold, and the sheep follow Him in a line.

5. You say, "The sheep hear His voice and follow Him. How they love to be with their Good Shepherd! He knows them, each one, their names, and what they are like. He loves each one just as they are because they are His, and He is theirs. He is their Good Shepherd." (All of the sheep are now standing inside the sheepfold.)

6. You say, "Now they are all together in the sheepfold—one family, one flock. How wonderful the

Good Shepherd is! They can trust Him. He will always lead and care for them. They feel so loved and protected. As night comes, He reminds them, *"I am the door. No one can go in and out except by me."* You say, "The Good Shepherd lies down across the doorway of the sheepfold. The sheep know that they can rest because he is taking care of them."

Meditation:
Wonderment:
You say, "I wonder what this all could mean...I wonder who this Good Shepherd really is...I wonder who the sheep might be...I wonder what this is all about..." (Be quiet and listen and wait.)

1. "I would like to tell you the secret of who the Good Shepherd is: His name is Jesus."

Prayer:
"Would you like to say something to the Good Shepherd?" Wait. Listen to their prayers.

1. After some of the children pray (if they do), then you can say, "Thank you, Good Shepherd, for loving me and bringing me into your family. Amen."

Worship Song:
"Let's sing a song that the sheep might sing: 'In God's Green Pastures Feeding,' (one verse)."

Closing:
"I will put this work back on the shelf. You may have a turn whenever you would like. This is a very special story. If you need a teacher to show it to you again, you may ask her."

"You may tell this story to another person or draw or write a story about the Good Shepherd."

Philosophy of the Lesson:

1. What is "wonderment"? Rather than delivering spiritual information to the children in a traditional didactic direct method, we value and respect the children's God-given discernment and strong propensity for understanding the heart of God. By trusting them (to a point) to understand, we honor the image of God within them and expect them to understand.

2. Why are the materials life-like, two-dimensional materials? These figures tell a parable that Jesus told, not a story about a real event in His life. Real stories will use three-dimensional figures, not two-dimensional ones. A parable uses items from life but is more abstract and can still use movement and give purpose to the story as well as more room for spiritual wonderment. Why do we take out parts of the parable when we read it to young children and only include the essential concepts or actions? (There is no mention of a "stranger," which would distract the children.) Non-essential concepts interfere in the understanding of children, ages two and a half to six or older, or even adults. So that listeners may understand easily, we eliminate non-essentials to the story and only emphasize one main point, called the "essentiality."

3. Why do we bother to use figures with children when we tell a story? Because children relate to visual stimuli and involve themselves in the story as if it were a real drama.

4. Why do we not state in the beginning that Jesus is the Good Shepherd? So that the children will

imagine and wonder who it might be and use their creative, God-given imaginations. And He will become real to them. Later they will chat together about who the Good Shepherd really is!

5. Why do we not tell them the name of the story at the beginning? Some children will say, "Oh, I know that one," or turn off their interest right away.

6. Why do we narrate some of the story and tell it from Jesus' own words for others? Because He says it best. His words are life to the story. But not all of the narrative is found literally in the Bible.

7. Why do we sometimes have the figures speak while they move, and other times we narrate or wait to move? Because the story is a drama, made to explain reality and thought, and must be in sequential order.

8. How important is it to pray and meditate all week as we prepare to show this lesson? Only God can anoint your storytelling and bring the main purpose to life. Because these lessons are so profound, it is hard for the teacher to give more than one lesson per week. The lessons require your very soul to be pulled and tugged within you.

9. What is the main purpose of the parable of the Good Shepherd? To introduce the children to a Person who loves them faithfully and completely by seeing the love of the Good Shepherd for His sheep. Maybe they have never really seen this kind of love before. It is your honor to tell them.

10. Is it important for the children to see that the sheep obey the Good Shepherd? The children's response

to pure love is obedience which is a necessary part of a full, abundant life.

11. How important are feelings of love, safety, faithfulness, and a supply of basic needs to children? They may be worrying about these things and need assurance of care.

12. Why do we ask them to "say something" rather than to pray? Because we want them to speak naturally to the Good Shepherd.

13. What is the importance of a song of worship that matches the lesson content? So that the child can feel and understand that God wants them to know the truths of this story in both words and music of the heart. Godly songs bring children's spiritual feelings to the surface.

14. How important is it for the child to be able to repeat this story just to himself or to another child? The freedom to retell the story in his own words brings more understanding and confidence in truly knowing it. The child will actually hold the small Bible, sometimes upside down, when beginning to tell the story to himself.

15. We must not jump years ahead and try to give conclusions to children that they cannot understand. Because the children will reenact these lessons, they will become very familiar with them over the years in class, and we will have many opportunities to lead them to the deeper theological concepts. We must trust God and not worry to the point that we try to cram many concepts into them when they are not ready.

Closing/Transition:

"Let's put this work away on the shelf. You may choose this work whenever you would like! This is a very special story. If you would like to ask a teacher to tell you the story again, you may. Perhaps you will find out more about who the Good Shepherd really is! Maybe you would like to draw or write a story about the Good Shepherd and His sheep."

Indirect Purpose:

To realize the deep, individual love Jesus has for each child shown by the fact that He knows our names; to learn that the Good Shepherd will really give His life for His sheep; to let the children know that the voice of the Good Shepherd (Jesus) can be heard and followed.

Lesson 2
The Found Sheep

Materials:
Same as the previous lesson.

Age:
Two and a half years and up.

Reading of Scripture:
Luke 15:4-7.

Direct Purpose:

To tell the children that the Good Shepherd loves His sheep so much that He will leave the others to go out to find the one that is lost. (By inference to let the children know that God loves them so much that He will always find them when they are lost, physically or spiritually.)

Presentation:

Say, "We remember the Good Shepherd and His sheep! The sheep had a good, quiet night's rest in their sheepfold, and the Good Shepherd slept by the door.

1. "In the morning, the Good Shepherd says, 'Good morning, my flock. Come! This is the day that the Lord has made. Let us rejoice and be glad in it! Follow me to the green grass where you can eat and lie down, and drink from the cool, nearby, quiet waters. Be sure to follow me closely and listen for my voice.' The Good Shepherd leaves the gate and moves toward the green pasture. The sheep follow Him, one by one, as He calls their names, to the pasture.

2. "Then He says, 'Follow me closely and listen for My voice.'

3. "The sheep know the voice of the Good Shepherd and want to follow closely behind Him.

4. "How the sheep love to be with their Good Shepherd! They are His, and He is theirs. He knows their names, each one, and loves and protects them! When evening comes, He calls them and says, 'Come, follow Me back to the sheepfold for the night. It is a safe, good place for you.' The sheep follow Him back to the fold, but one sheep strays

off the pasture and stays behind. Little Pete forgot to listen to the Good Shepherd's voice. He wanted to taste the juicy grass on the other side of the pathway. He wandered off by himself and got far away from the Good Shepherd.

5. "When the Good Shepherd and the sheep arrive back at the fold, the Good Shepherd counts his sheep. *'One is missing,'* he says. *'It is little Pete. I must go back and find him.'*

6. "The Good Shepherd leaves the fold and goes back to the pasture, calling, *'Little Pete! Come to me! Where are you?'* He heard a faint, 'Baa, baa,' and said again, *'Little Pete, come to me.'* He gave a special shepherd call and yelled his name louder, *'Pete, Pete,'* but he couldn't see him.

7. "Finally, he heard a quiet 'Baa, baa,' and looked over in the thorn and sticker bushes. *'There you are, little Pete. I have you now!'* The Good Shepherd reached down into the thorns and, with his rod and staff, pulled little Pete out from the thorny bush. He lifted him onto his shoulders and carried him home.

8. "The Good Shepherd was very happy. All of the sheep in the fold jumped and danced for joy and rejoiced that little Pete was not lost but was found. The Good Shepherd said, 'My *sheep that was lost is now found!'* All of the sheep lay down in the fold for the night, and the Good Shepherd lay down in front of the door to protect them."

Meditation:

1. "I wonder what this all could mean…I wonder why little Pete left the pathway…I wonder why one

sheep was so special..."

2. I wonder how little Pete felt when he was lost...I wonder why all of the other sheep were so happy...I wonder who the Good Shepherd really is... (Leave time to think between each wonderment.)

Prayer:
"Close your eyes very tight. If you have something to say to God, you may say it now." Wait. Listen to their prayers. Then pray yourself: "Dear God, thank you for finding me and bringing me home."

Worship Song:
"Surely Goodness and Mercy Shall Follow Me."

Conclusion/Transition:
"I will put this work back on the shelf, and you may use it. If you find out who the Good Shepherd really is, come and whisper in my ear so that I may know, too."

Philosophy of the Lesson:

1. Don't ask them but allow the children for a short while to tell about their experience getting lost and found and how they felt.

2. Do not articulate the purpose of the lesson in a traditional manner, but allow the Spirit of God to teach the children. Trust Him and trust the children's open spirit to God.

3. Do not be too dramatic or scary before the children.

Indirect Purpose:

To show the children that God keeps calling and calling us back. He even "carries" us when we cannot walk back. To show the children that the family of God loves each other and even rejoices when the lost one is found. This refers to the crucifixion of Christ through His reaching into the thorns and briars to get the sheep.

Lesson 3
The Announcement to Mary

Materials:

Wooden tray, basket of two three-dimensional figures, plain house, and house artifacts (Mary, angel [messenger], table, chair, loaf of bread, small basket of fruit, jug for water, and broom).

Paraphrased Reading of Scripture from Small Bible:

Luke 1:26-28. "Many, many years ago, something very exciting happened on this earth. I know that it is true because the Word of God tells the story."

Age:
Two and a half to six years and up.

Direct Purpose:
To tell the children that a baby king/savior was born to a young woman who said yes to God.

Presentation:

1. Say, "Once there was a lovely, young woman named Mary who was engaged to be married to a young man named Joseph. She lived in her parents' home and helped her mother by baking bread, carrying water from the well, and cleaning the house. I think that she was singing and praising God because she loved Him. Maybe she was thinking about the special Savior that God had promised would someday be born on earth. (Show Mary sweeping under the table with a broom and placing bread on the table, etc.)

2. "Suddenly, someone knocked on the door. *Knock, knock.* Mary opened the door and saw an angel (a messenger from God). (Mary opens the door, and the angel comes in.)

3. "The messenger said, 'Hello, Mary. You are very special to God. The Lord is with you and loves you.'"

4. Say, "Mary was worried. She thought, *Who is this person? What could his words mean?*" (The figure of Mary bends down.)

5. The messenger says, "Don't be afraid, Mary. God

has chosen you to become the mother of His Son. You will have a baby boy, and His name will be Jesus. He will become great, the greatest King that ever lived, and He will be the very Son of God. He will have a kingdom that will never end."

6. Say, "But Mary asked, 'How can this be? I don't have a husband.'"

7. He answered, "God's Spirit will begin the baby within you. The Holy Child will be called the Son of God!"

8. Say, "Mary thought and thought, and then she said, 'I love the Lord. I am His servant. I will do whatever God asks of me.'" Say, "Then the messenger leaves." (Angel exits.)

9. You: "Leave Mary in the house and follow with the Meditation steps."

Meditation:
Wonderment:
Say, "I wonder what this all could mean...I wonder how Mary felt when the messenger came to her house...How could a baby come to a young woman without a husband...I wonder why Mary said yes to God..."

Prayer:
Say, "Shut your eyes very tight. If you would like to say something to God, you may." Wait. Listen to their prayers.
"Dear God, thank you for choosing Mary, and that she said yes. Thank you for sending your Son Jesus to us. Amen."

Worship:
Say, "Let's sing a song that tells of Mary's love for God: 'I

Love You, Lord.'"

Conclusion/Transition:
Say, "I will put this work away now, and you may use it. If you would like a teacher to tell you the story again, you may ask her (or him)."

Philosophy of the Lesson:

1. Why do we use three-dimensional figures and not two-dimensional ones? When the event really happened, which Mary's visit did, then the three-dimensional figures make the story more real.

2. How much creative imagination can you use in the story? As long as you do not add extraneous items that might capture the child's imagination instead of the real purpose, you can add props within limits. Pick and choose what is most important in the story, but do not add nor emphasize peripheral details that distract from the purpose of the story.

3. Why do we sometimes say "messenger" rather than "angel"? Because children think of an angel with wings as a scary person. A messenger seems less frightening

4. The main purpose of this story for children is to know that Jesus had a human mother, chosen by God, who loved God and obeyed Him. Jesus came into this world as a human baby.

5. Why do we cover the work, before it is used, with a silk scarf? To keep the element of surprise, and to help the children keep listening to the scripture reading instead of looking at the figures.

6. This is the first of five "Birth of Jesus" narratives.

7. Why do we allow the children to reuse the materials? So that they may theologize in a childlike way and mull over in their hearts and spirit what happened.

8. Why do we show these lessons to two-and-a-half-year-olds? Because they will understand since we use figures but on a beginning level. Since we repeat the lesson to them each year or more often, they will build their understanding of the facts of the lesson and theological concepts each year.

Closing/Transition:
I will put this away, and you may use it. You may show yourself or another person the story. God will teach you more wonderful things.

Indirect Purpose:
To show children that God promised to send His Son to earth to become a king of an eternal kingdom. This was God's wonderful plan.

Lesson 4
The Announcement to the Shepherds

Materials:
Wooden tray, a small basket of three-dimensional materials, three to four shepherds, four to five sheep, green hard felt for pasture, three to five angels (messengers), and a silk scarf.

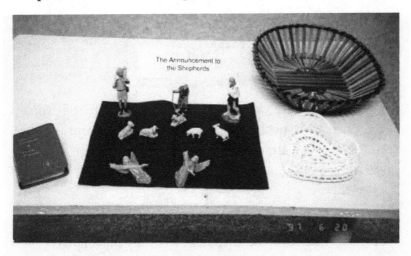

The Announcement to the Shepherds

Paraphrased Reading of Scripture:

"One day, many years ago, something very surprising happened on this earth. This had never happened before." Read Luke 2:8-20.

Age:

Two and a half to six years and up.

Direct Purpose:

To let the children know that God announced to the people of the earth with great joy that His Son is now born! (Try to keep this purpose utmost in your heart as you give the lesson.)

Presentation:

1. Say, "One dark night, some shepherds were taking care of their sheep out in a field when an angel appeared to them in the sky. (At least one shepherd was awake, but the others were sleeping.) It was a messenger from God." (The shepherds and the sheep are scattered out on the felt. Then hold at least two angels above them.)

2. Hold and read the Bible, *"A bright light shone above them, and the shepherds were very frightened."* (Lay the shepherds on their faces before the angels. Turn the sheep all to look at the angel.)

3. Then the angel said, "Don't be afraid! I bring you good news that will give you great joy for all people! Today in the nearby town of Bethlehem, a baby has been born! He is the Savior of the world! He is Christ, the Lord." Stand the shepherds up to look at the angels.

4. Read, "The angels say, 'This is how you will recognize Him: He will be born in a barn and sleeping in a cow's feeding basket. He will be wrapped up in a soft cloth. This is good news because He will save us from our sins.'"

5. Read, "Suddenly the sky was filled with many angels, all singing, 'Glory to God in the highest, and goodwill to all men.'" Bring all of the angels out while singing their song, "Jesus Christ is born today. Ah-ah-ah-ah-ah-le-lu-jah!" Make the shepherds once again fall down on their faces.

6. Then the angels leave. The shepherds stand up.

7. Say, "The shepherds look at each other and say, 'Let's go to Bethlehem and find this special baby that the Lord has told us about!' So they left several shepherds with their sheep, and some of them began walking to Bethlehem to find the newborn baby."

8. Move some shepherds off the green felt, walking away in a line toward the town.

Meditation:
Wonderment:

1. I wonder why God sent the angels to shepherds out in the field, taking care of sheep...

2. I wonder who this special baby really is that the angels are talking about...

Prayer:

1. "Would you like to say something to God? You may!" Wait and look at the children. Listen to their prayers.

2. Then say, "Dear God, thank you for sending your very own Son, baby Jesus, our Savior, to this earth. He is our Savior and Lord."

Worship Song:
"Jesus, Name Above All Names" (One verse).

Conclusion/Transition:
Say, "I will put this work away, and you may have a turn. Maybe you will find out who this special baby really is!"

Philosophy of the Lesson:

1. Keep the materials simple (only those listed). Note: When I first showed this work, I added a penlight above the angels flying to the field. When the children used the work, one of them put the angel on the penlight and said, "Here comes Luke Skywalker!" I never used a penlight again.

2. Realize that this is Act 1 for the shepherds and that the shepherds will reappear after the birth of Jesus.

They will become the first missionaries.

1. You might mention that God chose to first tell
   shepherds (poor, unimportant people) that His Son
   had been born.

   Indirect Purpose:
   To let children hear the term "Savior" and begin to think
   about what that means. To let them begin to think about
   "peace" and "joy" that will come through this baby boy.

Lesson 5
The Birth Of Jesus

Materials:

Wooden tray, simple manger or barn, Mary, Joseph, feeding basket, baby Jesus, donkey, cow, two shepherds, silver star on a piece of double dental floss, nail on the top of manger, and silk scarf. (Save shepherds and wise kings for their own lesson. Otherwise it gets to be too long for the children.)

Paraphrased Reading of Scripture:
Luke 2:1-7.

Age:
Two and a half years and up.

Direct Purpose:
To tell the children that God brought His Son here to earth for us! God took care of Mary and Joseph.

Presentation:
Say, "We remember the story of the visit of God's messengers to the shepherd in the fields. The angels came to the shepherds to tell them that a special baby boy had been born. Now we can find out the rest of the story from the Word of God."

1. Say, "One day, Joseph came to his engaged wife, Mary, and said, 'My dear Mary, the great king of Rome has said that everyone in the world must return to their home town to be counted. I must return to Bethlehem right away and bring you with

me. I will bring my father's donkey for you to ride when you are tired of walking. Can you be ready to go tomorrow?' he asked.

"'Yes, Joseph, it will be hard because the arrival of the baby is near, but I will go in the strength of the Lord. I will be ready.'

"Joseph replied, 'I will take care of you, and God will go before us.'"

2. Say, "The next morning, Joseph and Mary left their town of Nazareth and walked a very long way to another town, Bethlehem. They went up the hills and down the hills. At night they slept on the cold ground, and it took about two weeks to get there." (Move Joseph, Mary, and the donkey along the way to Bethlehem, and lay them down at night to rest with the donkey.)

3. Say, "As they came near to Bethlehem, Mary said, 'Joseph, please hurry. I think the baby is coming.'

"'Yes, Mary, I will go ahead and find a motel for us.' When he got there, Joseph went to the first motel he saw and knocked on the door. *Knock, knock.*" Say, "'Sir, do you have a room for me and my wife? She will have a baby soon.'

"'Sorry, sir,' replied the manager, 'We have no rooms left.'

"Joseph said, 'But, kind sir, my wife is very pregnant. We need a room very soon.'

"'There are no rooms here, mister.'

"Joseph said, 'Thank you anyway,' and he left."

4. Say, "Joseph hurried onto the next motel." (Repeat a second motel.)

5. Then say, "Joseph saw another motel down the road

and rushed there. He knocked on the door. *Knock, knock.* The manager opened the door and said, 'What do you want?'

"Joseph asked, 'Please, sir, my wife is going to have a baby soon. Do you have a room for us?'

"The manager replied, 'No, young man, we have been full for weeks. I am sorry—but wait a minute. There is a barn in the back for the cows and other animals. You may stay there tonight if you wish,' the manager added.

"'Thank you, thank you. We will, sir,' and Joseph hurried back to Mary and took her to the barn to rest for the night."

6. Say, "During the night, baby Jesus arrived." (Put the figure of baby Jesus onto the feeding basket. Have Him cry a small newborn cry.) "Mary and Joseph were so proud!" (Move them near the basket.) "They prayed, 'Thank you, dear God, for bringing baby Jesus here safely!'" (Move the cow and donkey near the baby and make their animal sounds: *moo, moo; hee-haw, hee-haw!*) Have Mary sing a short lullaby: "Away in a manger, no crib for a bed, the little Lord Jesus lay down His sweet head."

Meditation:
Wonderment:
"I wonder what this all could mean...I wonder who this special baby really is...I wonder how a baby who would become a king would be born in a barn..."

Prayer:
"Shut your eyes very tight. If you have something to say to God or to baby Jesus, you may say it now." Wait to let the children pray. Then say, "Dear God, thank you that Joseph took

good care of Mary, and so did you! Thank you for sending your very own Son to be born as a baby for us."

Worship Song:
"Jesus, Name above All Names."

Conclusion/Transition:
Say, "I will put this work away now. You may use it. Maybe you will find out why this baby is so special. Please come whisper in my ear if you find out!"

Philosophy of the Lesson:

1. Why can we imagine some background activities for Joseph and Mary that are not recounted in the Bible? To make the story more real. We know that many other discussions must have occurred between Joseph and Mary before the trip to Bethlehem.

2. Why do we want the children to notice that Joseph took care of Mary? To set a good example of a husband treating his wife.

3. Why do we make baby, cow, and donkey sounds? To bring life to the story.

4. Why do we suggest that the children might be able to find out why the baby is so special? To bring to light the fact that children often have insight into a spiritual story that the adult does not have.

Indirect Purpose:
To let the children see God's hand of protection and provision for the young family. To show the children that not everything was easy for them, but God was sovereign in His care for them.

Lesson 6
The Visit of the Shepherds

Materials:
Tray, manger, Mary, Joseph, baby Jesus in a small basket, cow, donkey, and two shepherds.

Reading of the Scripture:
Luke 2:15-20.

Age:

Two and a half to six years and up.

Introduction:

Say, "We remember when the angels visited the shepherds at night. We remember that the shepherds left their sheep to a few shepherds and went to visit the newborn king in Bethlehem."

Direct Purpose:

To tell the children that the shepherds went right out to proclaim the Good News on their way home.

Presentation:

1. Say, "The shepherds knew where the town of Bethlehem was and began walking there to find the special baby who was to become a king." (Move the shepherds along with the narrative.) "They arrived at the town of Bethlehem and went to the first motel. *Knock, knock.* The manager opened the door and said, 'Yes?'

    "The shepherds said, 'Sir, have you seen or heard of a baby born tonight in Bethlehem?'

    "He said, 'No, I haven't. We're busy. Goodbye.'"

2. Say, "The shepherds saw another motel a little further away and went there." (Move the shepherds along.) "They knocked—*knock, knock*—and the door opened. The manager said, 'Hello. We are having a party, but we have no rooms.'

    "The shepherds replied, 'That's okay, sir. We are not here for a party but are looking for a baby born tonight in this town.'

    "The manager answered, 'He's not here, and I don't know about him, goodbye.'"

3. Say, "The shepherds were disappointed but went on to the last motel and knocked on the door. *Knock, knock.* When the manager came to the door, he said, 'What do you want, shepherds?'

   "They said, 'We are looking for a baby born tonight in the town of Bethlehem. Have you seen or heard of him?'

   "The manager said, 'Yes, I have. I let a young couple spend the night in the back barn with the cows and donkeys, and I heard a baby cry. You may go to the back and find them.'

4. "The shepherds said, 'Oh, thank you very much!' And they ran to the back to the barn, and there was a young woman and man, with a newborn baby sleeping in a feeding basket, just as the angels had promised. The baby was so beautiful! The shepherds bowed down and praised God for the baby boy, Jesus, their Savior." (The two shepherds bow down.)

5. Say, "Then the shepherds thanked Mary and Joseph for letting them see the baby, and left the young couple, the baby, and the barn, telling everyone along the way, '*Baby Jesus, our Savior,* has been born today! He will be a king!' Everyone who heard them was amazed that this had happened! The shepherds kept telling everyone, '*Have you heard? Baby Jesus, the Son of God, has been born for you today!*' Or '*We saw Baby Jesus, our Savior, who has been born for you and for me. He will save us from our sins.*'"

Meditation:
Wonderment:
"I wonder what this visit of the shepherds really means…I wonder why the shepherds were so excited to see this baby…I wonder what kind of king He will become…How could He

take away their sins from the shepherds?"

Prayer:

This is your turn to say something to God if you would like. Listen to the prayers of the children. Wait. Listen to their prayers. Then you say, "Thank you, dear God, for sending this baby King to save us from our sins."

Worship Song:

"Go, Tell it on the Mountains" (one verse).

Interaction:

1. Take a shepherd to each child, put it in front of them, and say, "Beth, Did you know that Jesus, the Son of God, was born today for you?" Change the words a little as you go to put in each child's name and make it more interesting.

2. "I will return this work to the shelf for you to choose today."

Philosophy of the Lesson:

1. Notice the repetition of the search for a room, first by Joseph and then by the shepherds. This three-part repetition confirms the scenario to the children and makes it an interesting story. It is based on the same procedure that Joseph and Mary went through.

2. This narrative shows God's grace to humanity by choosing poor shepherds for His first announcement to people of the earth. God did not tell the rich and religious people.

3. The shepherds were the first missionaries.

Conclusion/Transition:

"I will put this work away, and you may have a turn. Please come whisper in my ear if you find out why the shepherds were so excited to tell others about the baby Jesus."

Indirect Purpose:

To show the children that it is good and natural to worship this special baby when you see Him. He will bring peace on earth and God's grace to all people. God is worthy of praise! Eventually, the children will learn that God loves simple shepherds and rich kings just the same.

Lesson 7
The Visit of the
Wise Kings

Materials:

Tray, house with windows, a picture, table and chair, basket of food, broom, Mary, Joseph, toddler Jesus (same tray as for the Birth of Jesus), camels (two if desired), three kings, chest of gifts (gold, frankincense and myrrh), and silver star with string (dental floss).

Reading of Scripture:

Let's read God's Word to see what happens next! Read Matthew 2:1-12.

Direct Purpose:

To show the children that God had the birth of His baby king all planned out ahead and also put a star in the sky for the kings to follow to find the new king.

Age:

Two and a half to six years and up.

Presentation:

1. Say, "Soon Joseph and Mary took their baby, Jesus, to a house where He grew and began walking. Show a one-year-old boy figure walking in the house. The house was in Bethlehem.

2. "Far away to a country in the East, three kings had been reading old Bibles and found out that a new king would be born in the town of Bethlehem when a bright star shone in the sky. For many months

the kings would sleep during the day and go out at night to search in the sky for a special star." (Bring out the kings several times, and back several times.) "Finally, one night, when they went out, they saw a new star and realized that it was the one that they had been looking for.

3. "They were so excited and saw that the star was moving. They hurried to follow it, having packed their bags and a chest of gifts for the new baby king. They followed the star many, many miles, across mountains and deserts, until they arrived in the city of Jerusalem where it disappeared. That was the city where King Herod lived. He was a very mean and jealous king and did not want anyone else to take his kingdom.

4. "The three kings went into Herod's palace and asked King Herod and his wise assistants if they had heard of a new king born in Bethlehem and if they had seen a new star in the sky. They said, 'No, but go to Bethlehem and search for this king and then come back and tell me where you find Him.' They hurried out toward Bethlehem, looked up to the sky, and saw the star again.

5. "The kings and their camels kept walking and following the star until it stopped over a house in Bethlehem." (Fasten the silver star onto the gable of the roofed house with a string of dental floss.) "The kings unpacked their gifts and went into the house to find the baby and His mother and adopted father. They were so happy to have found them!

6. "When they went into the house, they bowed down and worshipped the baby. They thanked God

for this new King Jesus." (Lay the kings down on their faces.) "They got up and opened the chest of gold, frankincense, and myrrh" (special perfumes and oils). Move the chest toward Mary and have them give the gifts to her and to Joseph.

7. "The three kings went to sleep that night, and, in the night, an angel warned them not to return to tell King Herod where the baby now was." (Show the angel over them as they sleep). "They returned to their far country." (Move the kings and camels down the road, away from the house.)

8. "A few nights later, God awoke Joseph in a dream, too, and said, 'Hurry to Egypt and take Mary and Jesus. King Herod is looking for the baby to harm Him.' So Joseph took Mary and Joseph far away during the night to the country of Egypt." (Move Joseph, Mary, Jesus, a donkey, and the chest away from the house.) "Mary and Joseph were very thankful for the gifts that the kings had brought them."

Meditation:
Wonderment:
"I wonder why God asked the kings to travel so far to find baby Jesus...I wonder what this all could mean...I wonder when Jesus will become king..."

Prayer:
"Shut your eyes very tight. If you would like to say something to God, you may." Listen to the prayers of the children, and then wait. Listen to the children's prayers. Then say, "Dear God, thank you for keeping baby Jesus safe. Thank you for sending us a new king."

Worship Song:
"Praise the Name of Jesus!"

Conclusion/Transition:

1. "I will put this work on the shelf, and you may use it. It is a very special work.

2. "If you would like a teacher to tell you the story again, please ask her."

Indirect Purpose:
To show the children that not everything was easy for them, but God was sovereign in His care for them. To show children that God speaks to us, sometimes in dreams. To show children that God loves His Son and protects Him. Years ago, God made plans for the stars to show the kings the way to Bethlehem.

Lesson 8
The Pearl of
Great Price

Materials:

Tray, open house with only a door, a three-dimensional table, a variety of jewels in three small jewelry boxes (with lids), a two-dimensional merchant figure, one large, shiny pearl in a lovely closed container, and small Bible.

The Pearl of Great Price

Reading of Scripture:
Read and paraphrase Matthew 13:45-46.

Age:
Two and a half to six and up.

Direct Purpose:

To show children that Jesus is the "Pearl of Great Price" who gives real joy and satisfaction to our hearts.

Presentation:

"Many years ago, when Jesus lived on this earth, He spoke about the kingdom of God. People asked Him, 'What is the kingdom of God?' Jesus told them a story."

1. Say, "Once there was a jeweler who had many beautiful jewels and pearls." (Place boxes of jewels on the table in the house, and stand the jeweler in front of them.)

2. "He was not happy. Even having all of these beautiful jewels did not make him happy. He *really* wanted to find the *one* most beautiful pearl in all the world. He wondered, *Where is it? How can I find it?*

3. "Every day, the jeweler left his home to go to the market to search for the *one* most beautiful pearl. (Lay a strip of hard tan felt at the side of the top of the table.) He walked up and down the streets, asking the storekeepers, 'Have you seen the one most beautiful pearl in all of the world?'" (Move the jeweler out the door of his house and to the open imaginary market, asking three imaginary merchants the same question.) "All of them said, 'No, sir, I have never seen or heard about that.'

4. "But every day he came home, so sad because he had not found the *one* most beautiful pearl in all of the world! He went into his house and looked at his jewels, but not one was the *one* he wanted. Every day he came out again, looking at the market for the pearl.

5. "Finally, one day, when the jeweler went to the market, he asked the storekeepers again, 'Have you ever seen a beautiful, large pearl?'

   "The last storekeeper answered, 'Yes, I have it in the backroom for you. Would you like to see it?'" (The storekeeper has no figure). Say, "The storekeeper left and brought the pearl out to show the jeweler. It was in a box, and the jeweler opened it.

   "The jeweler said, 'This is it! This is the most beautiful pearl in all of the world!'" (Open the lovely box and show the large pearl to the jeweler.)

6. "The jeweler said to the storekeeper, 'Please keep the pearl in the back safely for me. I will be right back to buy it. How much is it?'

   "The storekeeper answered, 'It is very expensive. It will take everything you own to buy it.'

   "The jeweler said, 'No matter. I must have this pearl. I will sell everything I have and return very soon to buy it.'

7. "The jeweler ran home and packed up all of his jewels. He went into his house, brought all of his jewels to the table and packed them in a few boxes, and rushed back to the market. He said, 'Please, sir, I am back and have brought you all of my jewels and pearls. I want to pay for the *one* pearl with everything that I have. May I have it?'

   "The storekeeper answered him, 'Yes, you may. I will sell you the *one* most beautiful pearl in the world for everything you have.'" Move the jewels and pearls away to the back of the imaginary market. Have the jeweler take the box with the pearl to his home.

8. "The jeweler opened the door to his house, went in and closed the door to his house, and sat at his

table. He put the box on the table and opened it, and took out the giant pearl and gazed at it. 'How beautiful this pearl is! It is so shiny and so large! I am finally happy! I will keep it always!'"

Meditation:
Wonderment:
"I wonder how the kingdom of heaven is like a jeweler who sells everything for one beautiful pearl...I wonder why the jeweler wanted this one pearl...I wonder what the pearl really is..."

Prayer:
"Shut your eyes very tight! If you would like to say something to God, you may say it now." (Wait.) Listen to the prayers of the children. "Dear God, thank you for bringing the kingdom of heaven to this earth and the *one* beautiful pearl! Amen."

Say, "I will tell you a secret. The *one* most beautiful pearl is Jesus."

Conclusion/Transition:
"I will put this work away, and you may tell the story to yourself or to others. Perhaps God will show you what this story really means. Maybe you would like to draw a picture of what this pearl might look like."

Indirect Purpose:
To show the children the great value of the kingdom of God and His Son, Jesus. God asks us to give our whole self to Him.

Philosophy:
God made beautiful things for us to enjoy, but to worship Him is the most beautiful thing of all.

Lesson 9
The Found Son

Materials:

Abstract house, father and two sons (son leaving the farm, then wearing old clothes, and next bending down), tree of pods, four pigs, son in fancy clothes and shoes, table, and chair.

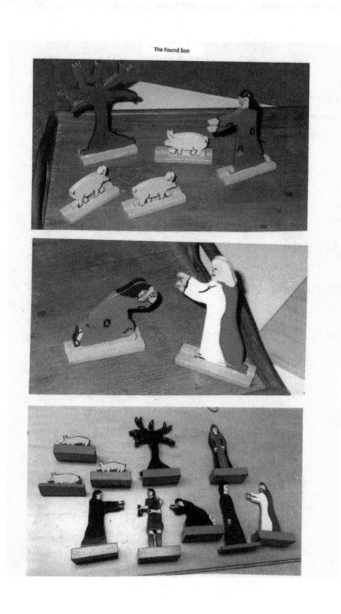

The Found Son

The Found Son

Reading of Scripture:
Luke 15:11-31.

Age:
Three years and up.

Direct Purpose:
To show children what God's unconditional (no conditions) love is like.

Presentation:

1. Say, "One day, someone asked Jesus why He liked to eat and be with people that others did not like. He said, 'I will tell you a story about two sons. One day the younger son asked his father, "Father, please give me my share of your money so that I can leave here. I am tired of working on this farm." The father did it.'

2. Say, "'Not too long after that, the son took his money and left to go to a far-off country. He had a wild time, spending his money on new friends and parties, but soon all of his money was gone. There was almost no food in the stores, and the son was hungry. The only place where he could find a job was taking care of pigs. He even wanted to eat the pigs' food, but no one would give him any.

3. "'Suddenly, he realized that his father had food on his farm. He decided to go home and ask his father to accept him back as a farmworker, not as a son. He went home.

4. "'The father loved his missing son and went out every day to look for him and to see if he might be coming home. No, his son was not there.

5. "'But before the son could even get to the house, his father saw him and ran out to greet him. The father threw his arms around the son and kissed him, and said, "O my son, I love you."

6. "'But the son said to his father, "Father, I have done wrong against God and you. I am not worthy of being called your son."

    But the father said, "Quick, bring the best robe

and put it on my son. Put a ring on his finger and sandals on his feet. Bring the best steak and let's have a party. My son, who was dead, is now alive. He was lost and is now found." And they began to celebrate.'"

7. Say, "'The older brother came to his father and said, "I worked hard for you, but you never gave me a party. My brother even took lots of money from you and left you, but you still celebrated his return."

His father answered, "Your brother was lost and is now found. He was dead and is now alive! My son, everything I have left is yours, but we must now rejoice!"'"

Meditation:
Wonderment:
"I wonder how the father felt when the young son left...I wonder how the young son felt when he was lost and hungry...I wonder how the father felt when he saw his son coming home...I wonder how the father felt when everyone but his older son was celebrating..."

Prayer:
"Would you like to say something to God now?" Listen to the prayers of the children. Wait. "Dear Father, thank you for forgiving and always loving us."

Worship Song:
"Thy Lovingkindness is Greater than Life."

Philosophy of the Lesson:

1. If you include two and a half to three-year-old children in the listening group, you might leave off the last scene with the older brother for a later time

in their lives. We must be true to the essentiality.

2. As the children use and reuse this work in their childhood, they will come upon other "aims" of the narrative, such as the forgiveness of sin by the father, even repentance, and selfishness. The story should be told again with an emphasis on each one of these concepts alone.

Indirect Purpose:
To learn how great the love of the father was. I wonder why it was so great…How is God's love like this?

Lesson 10
The Resurrection
(The Forever Life)

Materials:

Wooden tray, labels (beginning, middle, end, forever), a three-dimensional figure of Jesus in an opaque drawstring bag, small mirror, objects that are or have been alive (small plant, package of seeds, shell, raccoon tail, starfish, insect in a clear jar, real flower, etc.), lifetime book, and scarf.

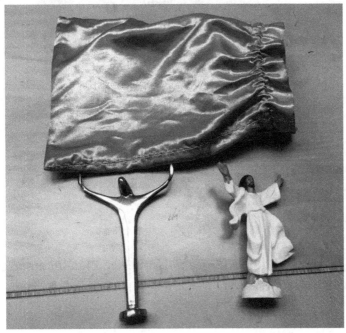

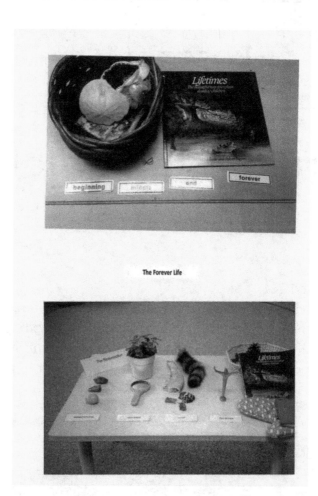

The Forever Life

Reading of Scripture:
John 11:25.

Age:
Two and a half years and up.

Direct Purpose:
To show children a special kind of forever lifetime that Jesus gives us.

Presentation:

1. Keep all of the materials under the silk cloth. Take out just the book and read it to the children, abbreviating some repetitive pages.

2. Close it, lay it down, and say, "This is a sad story. All living things will die someday.

3. "I will show you another story!" Lay out three of the four labels, left to right, at the front edge of the table. Read them as you go.

4. Take objects from the basket and look at each one, saying "beginning," "middle," or "end," and lay down near the correct label.

5. Take the figure of Jesus and place it near the "beginning" label. Say, "Jesus was born in Bethlehem." Place the Jesus figure near the "middle" label and say, "He lived and taught people and did many amazing things." But then move it to "end" and lay the figure down and say, "End. He died."

6. Then bring the figure of Jesus up and stand Him near the "forever" label. Say, "In three days Jesus came back to life again, and He made a new kind of lifetime, a 'forever' life!" Say, "one, two, three," and raise Jesus up. Then lay out the "forever" label.

7. Take the mirror, look into it, at your own face, and say, "beginning," (shake your head for no), "middle," (nod your head for yes), and move onto "end" and say, "No." Lay down the mirror under the "forever" label and say, "Forever." Now say, "Yes. I now have the forever life."

Meditation:
Wonderment:
"I wonder what kind of life the 'forever life' is…I wonder what this all could mean…I wonder who will be with me…"

Prayer:
"Shut your eyes very tight. If you would like to say something to God, you may do it now." Listen to the children's prayers. Wait. "Dear God, thank you for giving us the forever life! Amen."

Worship Song:
"I am the Resurrection and the Life!"

Conclusion/Transition:
"I will return this work to the shelf. You may choose it and find out more about the 'forever' life."

Indirect Purpose:
I wonder how long "forever" really is?

Lesson 11
The Found Coin

Materials:

Wooden tray, figure of the woman who lost a coin, figure of two neighbors, broom, lamp, table and chair, house, a necklace with nine coins, a single coin, and Bible.

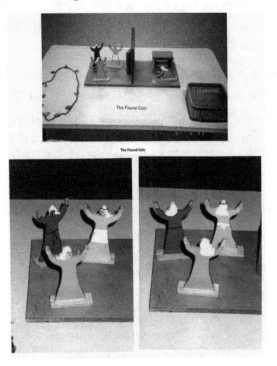

Reading of Scripture:
Luke 15:8-10.

Age:
Two and a half to six years.

Purpose:
To show children that God's great love seeks and finds us.

Presentation:

1. Say, "When Jesus was on this earth, He loved to talk about the kingdom of God. He told this story, 'Once there was a woman who had ten beautiful coins,'" (show the necklace of nine coins) "'she wore at her wedding. One day she lost one coin. She counted them again.'" (Lay the necklace out flat and count the coins.) "'She said, "Oh no, there are only nine coins here! I must find the one missing coin!" She missed it very much!'"

2. Say, "'So she took a lamp and lit it and looked in every corner of her house, under the table and chair and everywhere, but it was not there! Then she got her broom and carefully swept the floor and every corner. She could not find it! Oh, what shall she do?

3. "'Suddenly, she saw a sparkle under the table. She bent down, and there it was! Her lost coin was found!'"

4. Lay out the necklace and put the "found coin" in its place.

5. "'She went out and called her friends and neighbors and said to them, "I am so happy! I found my lost coin! Let's celebrate! Please come over and have a party! Be happy with me! I have found my lost coin!"'" Bring two neighbors over to rejoice. "'They all danced and sang and were happy!'"

Meditation:

Wonderment:

I wonder what this all could mean...I wonder why she missed the one coin she lost so much...I wonder what Jesus means when He says, "Just like this, the angels of God in heaven rejoice when one lost child comes back home..." Wait and listen to the children.

Prayer:

"Close your eyes very tight. If you have something to say to God, you may say it now." Listen to the children's prayers. "Dear Father, thank you for finding me and bringing me into your family. Amen."

Worship Song:

"I will enter His gates with Thanksgiving in my heart."

Conclusion/Transition:

"I will put this work away on the shelf. You may choose it and use it. Perhaps God will tell you more about why everyone was so excited about the found coin and what this really means!"

Indirect Purpose:

To show children another kind of "lost and found" story and how important we all are in the kingdom of heaven.

Philosophy:

Through the concept of "Lost and Found" in all three lessons (Found Sheep, Found Son, and Found Coin), the children will understand how God's great love searches for us when we are lost and finds us.

Lesson 12
Creation

Materials:

Tray with circular picture cards depicting the seven days of creation story, rectangular narrative cards describing the seven days of creation and rest narrative, labels for the seven days, basket of solar system objects, and plants and animals.

Creation

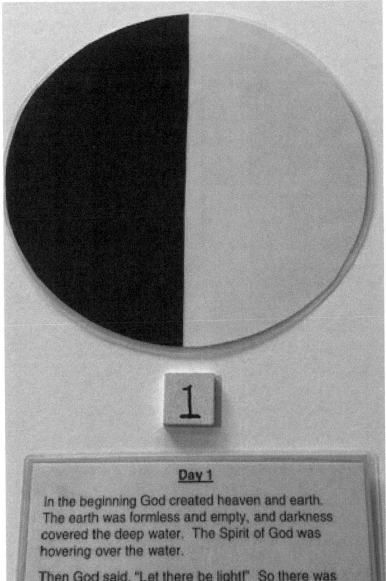

Day 1

In the beginning God created heaven and earth. The earth was formless and empty, and darkness covered the deep water. The Spirit of God was hovering over the water.

Then God said, "Let there be light!" So there was light. God saw the light was good. So God separated the light from the darkness. God named the light <u>day</u>, and the darkness he named <u>night</u>. There was evening, then morning---the first day.

Day 2

Then God said, "Let there be a horizon in the middle of the water in order to separate the water." So God made the horizon and separated the water above and below the horizon. And so it was. God named what was above the horizon <u>sky</u>. There was evening, then morning---a second day.

Day 3

Then God said, "Let the water under the sky come together in one area, and let the dry land appear." And so it was. God named the dry land <u>earth</u>. The water which came together he named <u>sea</u>. God saw that it was good. Then God said, "Let the earth produce vegetation: plants bearing seeds, each according to its own type, and fruit trees bearing fruit with seeds, each according to its own type. And so it was. The earth produced vegetation: plants bearing seeds, each according to its own type, and trees bearing fruit with seeds, each according to its own type. God saw that they were good. There was evening, then morning---a third day.

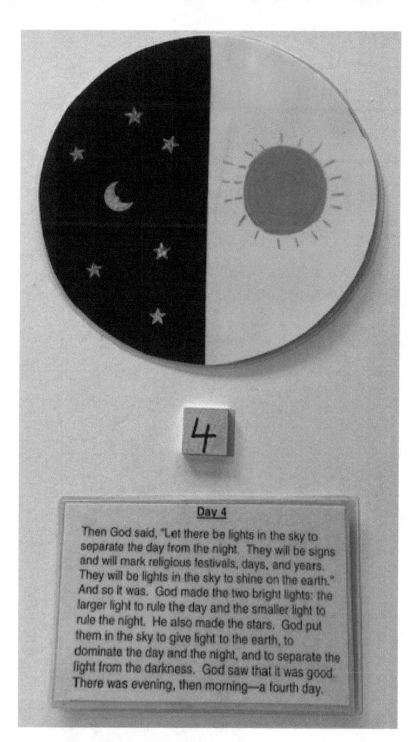

4

Day 4

Then God said, "Let there be lights in the sky to separate the day from the night. They will be signs and will mark religious festivals, days, and years. They will be lights in the sky to shine on the earth." And so it was. God made the two bright lights: the larger light to rule the day and the smaller light to rule the night. He also made the stars. God put them in the sky to give light to the earth, to dominate the day and the night, and to separate the light from the darkness. God saw that it was good. There was evening, then morning—a fourth day.

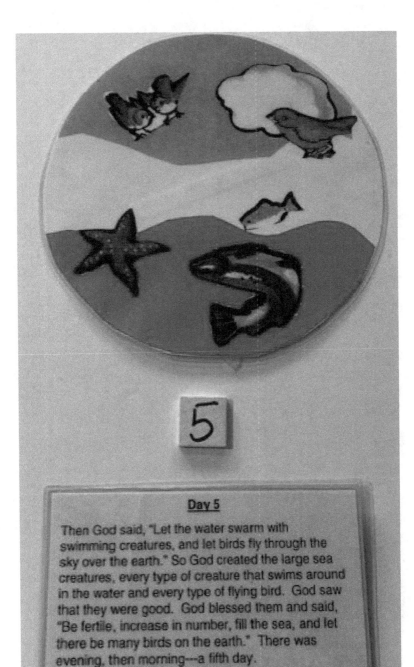

Day 5

Then God said, "Let the water swarm with swimming creatures, and let birds fly through the sky over the earth." So God created the large sea creatures, every type of creature that swims around in the water and every type of flying bird. God saw that they were good. God blessed them and said, "Be fertile, increase in number, fill the sea, and let there be many birds on the earth." There was evening, then morning---a fifth day.

Day 6

Then God said, "Let the earth produce every type of living creature: every type of domestic animal, crawling animal, and wild animal. And so it was. God made every type of wild animal, every type of domestic animal, every type of creature that crawls on the ground. God saw that they were good.

Then God said, "Let us make humans in our image, in our likeness. Let them rule the fish in the sea, the birds in the sky, the domestic animals all over the earth and all the animals that crawl on the earth."

So God created humans in his image.
In the image of God he created them.
He created them male and female.

God blessed them and said, "Be fertile, increase in number, fill the earth, and be its master. Rule the fish in the sea, the birds in the sky, and all the animals that crawl on the earth."

God said, "I have given you every plant with seeds on the face of the earth and every tree that has fruit with seeds. This will be your food. I have given all green plants as food to every land animal, every bird in the sky, and every animal that crawls on the earth---every living, breathing animal." And so it was.

And God saw everything that he had made and that it was very good. There was evening, then morning---the sixth day.

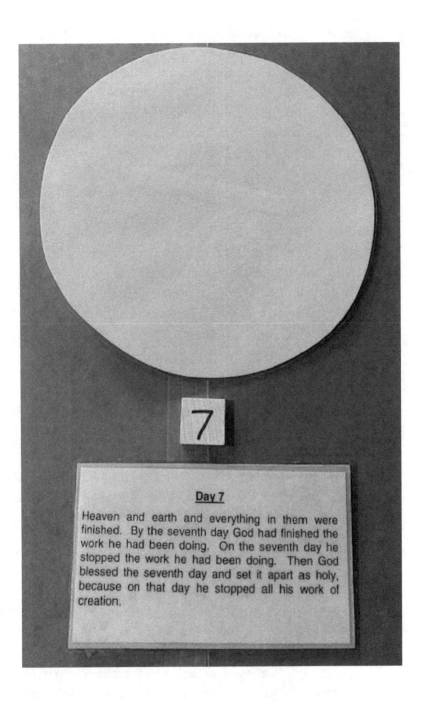

Day 7

Heaven and earth and everything in them were finished. By the seventh day God had finished the work he had been doing. On the seventh day he stopped the work he had been doing. Then God blessed the seventh day and set it apart as holy, because on that day he stopped all his work of creation.

Day 1:

In the beginning God created heaven and earth. The earth was formless and empty, and darkness covered the deep water. The Spirit of God was hovering over the water.

Then God said, "Let there be light!" So there was light. God saw the light was good. So God separated the light from the darkness. God named the light "Day" and the darkness "Night."
There was evening, then morning---the first Day.

Day 2:

Then God said, "Let there be a horizon in the middle of the water in order to separate the water."
So God made the horizon and separated the water above and below the horizon. And so it was. God named what was above the horizon, "Sky." There was evening, then morning ---a second Day.

Day 3:

Then God said, "Let the water under the Sky come together in one area, and let the dry land appear." And so it was. God named the dry land "Earth." The water which came together he named "Sea." God saw that it was good. Then God said, "Let the earth produce vegetation: plants bearing seeds, each according to its own type, and fruit trees bearing fruit with seed, each according to its own type." And it was so. The Earth produced vegetation: plants bearing seeds, each according to its own type, and trees bearing fruit with seeds, each according to its own type. God saw that they were good. There was evening, then morning--a third Day.

Day 4:

Then God said, "Let there be lights in the Sky to separate the Day from the Night. They will be signs and will mark religious festivals, days and years. They will be lights in the Sky to shine on the Earth." And so it was. God made the two bright lights: the larger light to rule the Day, and the smaller light to rule the Night.

He also made the Stars. God put them in the Sky to give light to the Earth, the Sun to dominate the Day and the Moon to dominate the night, and to separate the light from the darkness. God saw that it was good. There was evening, then morning--a fourth Day.

Day 5:

Then God said, "Let the water swarm with swimming creatures, and let birds fly through the Sky over the Earth." So God created the large Sea creatures, every type of creature that swims around in the water and every type of flying bird. God saw that they were good. God blessed them and said, "Be fertile, increase in number, fill the Sea and let there be many birds on the Earth" There was evening, then morning--a fifth Day.

Day 6:

Then God said, "Let the Earth produce every type of living creature: every type of domestic animal, crawling animal and wild animal. And so it was. God made every type of creature that crawls on the ground. God saw that they were good.

Then God said, "Let us make humans in our image, in our likeness. Let them rule the fish in the Sea, the birds in the Sky, the domestic animals all over the Earth and all the animals that crawl on the Earth."

So God created the Humans in his image. In the image of God he created them, He created them male and female. God blessed them and said, "Be fertile, increase in number, fill the Earth, and be its master. Rule the fish in the Sea, the birds in the Sky, and all the animals that crawl on the Earth."

God said, "I have given you every plant with seeds on the face of the Earth and every tree that has fruit with seeds. This will be your food. I have given all green plants as food to every land animal, every bird in the Sky, and every animal that crawls on the Earth--every living, breathing animal." And so it was.

And God saw everything that he had made and that it was very good. There was evening, then morning--the sixth Day.

Day 7:
Heaven and Earth and everything in them were finished. By the seventh Day God had finished the work he had been doing. On the seventh Day he stopped the work he had been doing. Then God blessed the seventh Day and set it apart as holy, because on that Day he stopped all his work of creation.

Age:
Two and a half years and up.

Paraphrased Reading of Scripture:
Selected parts of Genesis 1 and 2.

Direct Purpose:
To tell children the true story of God's creation of the world.

Say, "Many people in our world ask important questions like, 'How did this world get here? Who made it, and how did all of the sun, moon, stars, plants, animals, and people get here? How did I get here?'"

Presentation:
Say, "In the Bible, God told us a wonderful story about how this all happened. Watch. This is how it happened."

1. Lay out the seven numeral cards at the top, from left to right on the long rug, reading the numerals as you go, preparing a seven-place lateral organization with space for the circles, and read, "Day one, day two, etc." through day seven.

2. Prepare the seven circular pictures to be in order in a stack. Take the top one and place it below the numeral card, reading "Day one." Continue through seven.

3. Prepare the seven rectangular reading cards to be in order (to avoid confusion), upside down in a stack on the left.

4. Take the top card, read it, and lay it under the first circle. Continue taking one card at a time, reading it, and laying it beneath the appropriate circle.

5. Lay out all of the objects from the basket to the table.

6. Begin again with day one and point and say what God made that day. Find that object and lay it beneath the picture circle cards.

7. Put your hands in your lap and admire the work of God in creation. Say, "On day seven, God rested."

Meditation:
"I wonder how God could make so many beautiful things in a short time..."

Prayer:
"Shut your eyes very tight. If you have anything to say to God, you may say it now." Listen to the children's prayers. Wait. Then you pray, "Dear God, thank you for making everything in the world so beautiful, even me!"

Worship Song:
Sing all verses of "He's Got the Whole World in His Hands."

Conclusion/Transition:
"I will put away this work, and you may have a turn. If you discover how all of this happened, please come and whisper in my ear so that I may know, too."

Indirect Purpose:
To think about what God made on each day.

Philosophy:
This lesson shows the great, creative work of God in the cosmos and divides it into seven days for the children to try to comprehend the labor of each day by God. This is a basic, deep-seated question for all children who need to see and hear God's view of creation.

Lesson 13
The Ten Secrets
to a Happy Life

Materials:
Moses figure, Ten Commandments in stone replica, and heart-shaped tray with puzzle commandments inside.

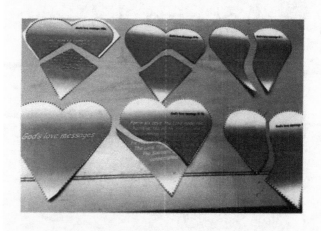

The Ten Secrets of a Happy Life

Age:
Four years and up.

Reading of Scripture:
Exodus 20 and 32. "God loved His people so much that He wanted to tell them secrets of how to live a happy life. One day He told Moses, a man of God, what the ten secrets to a happy life are."

Direct Purpose:
To help children receive God's wonderful gift of happiness through knowledge of right and obedience.

Presentation:

1. "One day, God decided that He would tell His people what the ten secrets to a happy life are. Moses loved God and wanted to follow Him. He listened to God, and God told him to come to the mountaintop with Him." (Move the Moses figure to a mountain shape higher than the table.)

2. God said, "Moses, I am the Lord your God. I will give you ten secrets for a happy life to tell to your people.

3. "Number 1: Remember that I, alone, am your God.
   "Number 2: Do not bow down and worship anything that you make.
   "Number 3: Do not use my name as a swear word.
   "Number 4: Remember to rest and worship Me one day a week.
   "Number 5: Honor and obey your mother and your father.
   "Number 6: Do not kill anyone.
   "Number 7: Have only one wife or husband.
   "Number 8: Do not steal other people's belongings.
   "Number 9: Do not lie about anyone.
   "Number 10: Do not put your eye on other people's belongings and try to get them."
   Say, "God Himself wrote these ten secrets onto two stone tablets, front and back.

4. "Let's see if we can put these puzzles of the ten secrets together." (Lay out all ten upper puzzle pieces
   on the top half of the table and ten lower pieces on
   the lower half of the table.) Looking for the first
   commandment in numerical order, read and put
   together each completed commandment as you go.

Meditation:
Wonderment:
I wonder how these ten secrets can bring a happy life...I
wonder how God wrote them on the stone tablets...I wonder
why He gave these secrets to us...

Prayer:
"If you would like to say something to God, you may." Listen to the children's prayers. Wait. "Thank you for your love.
You know us the best. Thank you for giving us these ten secrets
so that we can be very happy."

Worship Song:
"Thy Word Is a Lamp unto My Feet."

Conclusion/Transition:
Maybe you would like to make a rubbing of the ten secrets
from the stone with crayon and paper.

Indirect Purpose:
To put children on the path of righteousness.

Philosophy:
This lesson makes the commandments of God a gift of
guidance for us for a good and better life than without them.
These are His special secrets for us to follow His path for
our lives.

Lesson 14
The Good Friend

Materials:

Wooden figures (beaten man [walking and lying on ground], choir director, priest, stranger from another country, donkey, motel owner, and parable house).

The Good Friend

Age:
Four years and up.

Reading of Scripture:
Luke 10:30-36.

Purpose:
To show children who their neighbor really is (whom Jesus says to love as themselves).

Presentation:

1. "One day, a lawyer came up to Jesus and asked Him a trick question, 'Teacher, what must I do to go to heaven?'

2. "Jesus answered, 'What does the Bible say?'
   "The man answered, 'Love the Lord your God with all of your heart, with all of your soul, with all of your strength, and with all of your mind, and love your neighbor as yourself.'

3. "Jesus said, 'You are right.'
   "But the lawyer asked him again, 'Who is my neighbor?' Jesus answered him with a story.

4. "'Once there was a man who was going from one city to another when robbers stopped and attacked him, beat him up, and left him for dead.

5. "'Then it happened that a pastor was going down that same road. He saw the man and walked away to the other side of the road.

6. "'Next, a church song leader came by the beaten man along the road. The musician went over and looked at the man but then walked away to the other side of the road.

7. "'But a stranger from another country was also traveling on the same road, saw the hurt man, and

his heart was filled with pity for him. The stranger went over to the man, poured oil and wine on his wounds, bandaged them, and put the man on his own donkey to take him to a motel. He asked the motel manager to take care of him, gave him two silver coins, and said, "Please take care of this man for me, and when I return this way again, I will repay you whatever you spend on him.'"

8. "Then Jesus asked the lawyer, 'Which of these three men acted like a good neighbor toward the man who was attacked?'

9. "The lawyer replied, 'The one who was kind to him.'

10. "Then Jesus said to him, 'Go and do the same!'"

Meditation:
Wonderment:
I wonder what this could all mean...I wonder why the priest and song leader did not help the man...I wonder why the stranger would help him...I wonder what it is like to help your neighbor...

Prayer:
"If you would like to say something to God, you may say it now." Wait. Listen to the children's prayers. "Dear God, please help us to be kind to those who are hurt. Help us be ready to help. We want to enter the kingdom of heaven."

Worship Song:
"O, I Love You with the Love of the Lord."

Conclusion/Transition:
"I will put this work away, and you may have a turn. Let me know if God tells you more about what real love is."

Indirect Purpose:

To show children how to choose to love another person.

Philosophy:

By showing how a stranger can save the life of a broken man, without any recompense at all, in contrast to two officials who should love, causes children to think in caring ways about helping others.

Lesson 15
The Parable of Prayer

Materials:

Parable house, persistent friend, three small loaves of bread, neighbor and wife, bunk bed, and traveling friend.

Reading of Scripture:
Luke 11:5-10.

Age:
Four years and up.

Direct Purpose:

To show the child that it is good to keep asking, seeking, and knocking when you pray.

Presentation:

1. "One day, Jesus' friends asked Him how they should pray. Then He taught them a simple, beautiful prayer and said, 'Now I will tell you a story about prayer.' He said, 'Once there was a man who went to his neighbor's house at midnight and knocked on the door.' *Knock, knock.* 'Dear neighbor, may I please borrow three loaves of bread? My friend is coming from a long trip, and I have no food to give him.'

    "'And suppose his friend inside the house said, "Don't bother me! My door is already locked, and my children and I are in bed. I can't get up and give you anything."

2. Say, "Jesus said, 'I tell you, even though he won't get up and give you bread because the man is his friend, he will get up and give you everything you need because you are not ashamed to keep on asking. For I say to you, "Ask, and you shall receive, seek, and you will find. Knock, and the door will be opened to you. For those who ask will receive, those who seek will find, and the door will be opened to anyone who knocks."'" Say, "This is what prayer is like."

3. Make the three puzzle pieces in three different colors, cut the puzzles in the middle of each, and spread them out on the table. Find the "Ask" first half and then its last half partner and slide them together. Read it.

4. Take the "Seek" first half and then its last half partner and slide it together. Read it.

5. Take the "Knock" first half and then its last half partner and slide it together. Read it.

6. "Jesus said, 'If your father on earth loves you so much to give you many good things, how much more will your heavenly Father give you what you ask.'"

Meditation:
Wonderment:
"I wonder how prayer is like asking your neighbor for bread...I wonder why the man in the house finally got up and gave three loaves of bread to his neighbor...I wonder how this story is like prayer to God...I wonder what it means to ask, to seek, and to knock when you pray..."

Prayer:
"Would you like to say something to God about this story?" Listen to the children's prayers. Wait. "Dear Jesus, thank you for telling us that you answer our prayers and to keep praying and praying. I will do that."

Worship Song:
"Seek You First the Kingdom of God."

Conclusion/transition:
"I will put this work away, and you may have a turn. Maybe you will figure out why the neighbor gave him the three loaves of bread..."

Indirect Purpose:
To show children that God loves to have us talk with Him.

Philosophy:

Children will be happy to find out that it is good to ask and keep asking, to seek and keep seeking, and to knock and keep knocking because that's what they do in real life. So they can do it in prayer.

Lesson 16
The Four Soils

Materials:

An empty bowl, a medium-sized bowl of good soil, same size bowl of the following: hard soil, rocks, small sticks and thorns (with labels taped on the side), strainer to fit the bowls, spoon, eye-dropper, cup of water, newsprint, and small Bible. A package of small seeds. Four small story labels: hard soil, rocky soil, thorny soil, good soil.

Reading of Scripture:
Matthew 13:1-9.

Age:
Three years and up.

Direct Purpose:
The kingdom of God is similar to people with hearts like four kinds of soil: Hard, rocky, thorny, and good, fine soil.

Presentation:

1. "When Jesus lived on this earth, he told this story." Say, "The kingdom of heaven is like a man who went out to sow grain. As he scattered some in the field, some of it fell along the path, and the birds came and ate it up." Show the hard soil. "This soil is like a person's heart which is hard and is not open to God." Show the correct bowl of soil as you give the narrative.

2. "Some of it fell on the rocky ground where there was little soil. The seeds soon sprouted because the soil wasn't deep. But when the sun came up, it burned the young plants, and because the roots had not grown deep enough, the plants soon dried up." Show the correct bowl of soil. Say, "This soil reminds us of the person's heart which is happy to receive it but does not sink deep into Him. When trouble comes, he gives up."

3. "*Some of the seed fell among thorn bushes which grew up and choked the plants.*" Show the proper bowl of soil. Say, "This soil reminds us of the heart that loves the worries of life and riches, which choke out the message and does not bear fruit."

4. "But some seeds grew in good soil, and the plants bore grain: some had one hundred grains, others

sixty and others thirty. Listen, if you have ears to hear." Show the bowl of good soil. Say, "This soil reminds us of the heart that hears God's message, understands it, and bears much fruit. Feel the softness of the good soil."

5. "Let's see what these four kinds of soil look like."

6. Take the bowl of hard soil and pour it into the empty bowl. Feel and examine it. Put the strainer over the "good" bowl and pour the soil into the strainer. 'Let's see if we can make any good soil?' Whatever good soil goes through the strainer, pour it into the good soil bowl. Pour the hard soil back into the hard soil bowl. This soil reminds us of the heart that hears God's message but is not open to God.

7. Take the bowl of rocky soil and pour it into the empty bowl. Feel and examine it. Put the strainer over the "good" bowl and pour the soil into the strainer. "Let's see if we can make any good soil?" Whatever good soil goes through the strainer, pour it into the good soil bowl. Pour the rocky soil back into the rocky soil bowl. This soil reminds us of the heart that is happy to receive the message, but it does not sink deep into him. When trouble comes, he gives up.

8. Take the bowl of thorny soil and pour it into the empty bowl. Feel and examine it. Put the strainer over the "good" bowl and pour the soil into the strainer. Let's see if we can make any good soil. Whatever good soil goes through the strainer, pour it into the good soil bowl. Pour the thorny soil back into the thorny soil bowl. This soil reminds us of the heart that hears the message but loves the wor-

ries of life and riches and does not bear fruit.

9. Take a small empty clear glass container and say, "This good soil reminds me of the person's heart who receives the message of God, understands it, and bears fruit. I will make myself a good soil container to put into my window with two seeds in it." Take a spoon and fill the small container half-full of soil.

10. Put two seeds into it and get water in the eye-dropper and count two drops of water into your container. I will put it onto my window sill and water it every other day with the eye-dropper and think about the story of the good soil.

Meditation:
Wonderment:
"I wonder what this all could mean...I wonder what kind of soil my heart is..."

Prayer:
"Shut your eyes very tight. If you would like to say something to God, you may." Listen to the children's prayers. Wait. "Dear God, Open my heart and help me understand your Word."

Worship Song:
"Father, I Adore You."

Conclusion/Transition:
"I will clean and pack up all of this work so that you may use it. I will return it to the shelf for you. Please whisper in my ear if you learn some new things about God!"

Indirect Purpose:

To show children that the 'soil' of our heart may need to be changed to grow good plants.

Philosophy:

Feeling the soft, malleable, warm soil, compared with the other three soils, shows the children a real picture of what their good heart should be like.

Lesson 17
The Mustard Seed

Materials:

A small brown hard felt, a small beautiful container with tiny black seeds, a tree about 8 inches tall with lovely leaves and trunk, two-dimensional figure of a farmer, small basket with lid, and five small feathered birds inside with two wires each for legs. For older children, make "gifts to humanity" labels with sticks to put into the tree: *kindness, peace, hospitals, schools, no slavery, freedom, women's and children's rights, equality, creative thinking, one wife or husband, fair laws, adoption, justice, righteousness, hospitality, democracy, charity, morality, respect.*

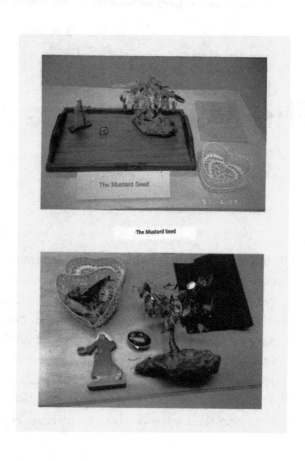

The Mustard Seed

The Mustard Seed

Reading of Scripture:
Matthew 13:31-32.

Direct Purpose:
To show children the grand and great plan of the kingdom of God expanding throughout the whole world from one tiny seed to a "tree" that gives healing, love, goodness, and grace to the whole world.

Age:
Four years and up.

Presentation:

1. "Jesus told His friends another parable of the king-
    dom of God. A man takes a mustard seed and sows
    (plants) it in his field. (It is the smallest seed in
    the world.)." Open the small container of seed and
    place one on the brown felt. Say, "The man waited
    and waited for the seed to sprout and to grow to its
    full height." Remove the seed container to the area
    of the materials on the edge of the table.

2. Bring out the beautiful tree and place it on the
    felt. Say, "This tree grew so tall and beautiful from
    the smallest seed in the world. Its leaves were so
    strong and lovely that many birds of the air came
    and made their nest in its branches. They wanted
    to have shade and safety." Open the basket of birds
    and "fly" each one to a branch of the tree to stay
    there. Say, "The birds will make their nests there in
    the shelter and safety of this tree."

3. From one tiny seed, the tree (kingdom of God) will
    grow to become the greatest gift to all of the world
    of goodness and love.

Meditation:
Wonderment:
"I wonder how a very tiny seed could grow into a tree...I
wonder what made it grow so large...I wonder what or who
the seed really is...I wonder who the farmer is...I wonder what
kind of special tree this really is...How could this seed and tree
be like the kingdom of heaven...?"
Using the lovely seed box, put a small amount of ground

pepper into it, ask each child to put out his hand, and give him a few "seeds." Say, "These tiny pieces remind us of mustard seeds." (They are so tiny that they are nearly indistinguishable from the seeds and get lost in their hand. This impresses the child, how very tiny the seed really is and how marvelous that it can grow as large as a tree. It becomes evident that it is a God-inspired growth.)

Prayer:
"Would you like to say something to God now?" Wait. Listen to the children's prayers. Wait.

Pray, "Dear God, thank you for the seed of Jesus. Thank you for the wonderful kingdom of heaven on earth and all of the gracious goodness it brings to our world."

Worship Song:
"Jesus, Name Above All Names."

Conclusion/Transition:
"I will put this work away, and you may have a turn. Please come whisper in my ear if you find out more about this wonderful tree."

Philosophy of the Lesson:

1. Be aware that the mustard seed is not the large, yellow seed often found in Christian jewelry. When my husband and I were in Israel and came out of the Capernaum church, a group of nuns were carrying branches, and I asked, "What are those?"

   They answered, "mustard seeds." I asked where they got them, and they said, "On the fence outside of the churchyard." For days we had been looking along the roads for them and asking our bus driver, but he did not know.

So we rushed over and pulled off as many as we could get and took them into our bus. We harvested the seed pods in our hotel room and took them home to use in our school. Dr. Sofia Cavalletti, the author of *The Catechesis of the Good Shepherd*, had mustard seeds growing in window boxes in her apartment in Rome and later gave us a mustard seed plant for the US. The seeds are black and very small.

2. In order to simplify the lesson, we do not put nests under the birds in the tree.

3. It works well to sprinkle ground black pepper into the seed box and use that instead of real seeds.

4. When showing this to older children and adults, discuss with them your research on the impact of the Gospel in the world: churches, hospitals, schools, orphanages, charities, etc., as well as "peace" in a secular world, and make stick labels for the tree of these concepts.

Indirect Purpose:
To meditate on the grace that the gospel brings to heal our often difficult world.

Lesson 18
The Leaven

Materials:
A two-dimensional figure of a woman, miniature bowl and miniature sack of flour, one large clear bowl, small sack of real flour, package of dry yeast, small pitcher for water, one wooden mixing spoon, mixing cloth, covering cloth, sink or bowl nearby for washing hands, labels: flour, yeast, water, strainer, small jars, and newsprint.

Direct Purpose:
To meditate with the children to try to understand how yeast makes flour as the kingdom of God is to our world.

Age:
Five years old and up.

Reading of Scripture:
Matthew 13:33.

Presentation:
"Many years ago, when Jesus lived on this earth, He said so many interesting things about the kingdom of heaven. The Word of God tells us that He told this story about the kingdom of heaven." Show the figure of the woman, the small package of flour, and the pitcher:

1. Then say, "Jesus said, 'The kingdom of God is like a woman who takes some yeast and mixes it into a bushel of flour until the whole batch of flour rises.'" Open the real sack of flour, put the large bowl in front of you, and pour all of the flour into the large bowl.

2. Get a large cup full of warm water, pour the dry yeast into the cup, and stir the mixture.

3. Pour the yeast mixture into the bowl of flour and begin mixing it into the flour with the wooden spoon. Say, "Let's mix in the yeast as Jesus said that the woman did." Mix with your hands until the batch is nearly mixed.

4. Mix until the yeast is almost evenly dispersed through the whole batch of flour. Allow children to wash their hands, put some flour on their hands, and come have a turn to knead the mixture on the cloth. Put the batch out onto the mixing cloth.

5. When the children are done, remove the flour/yeast mixture intact back to the bowl. Cover the bowl with a clean cloth.

6. Say, "Let's put this bowl in a warm place and watch to see what will happen. We must be careful not to touch the mixture."

7. After several hours, sing the walking music and bring the children back to the circle. Bring the raised bowl of flour/yeast mixture with its cloth over it.

Meditation:
Say, "I wonder what has happened to the flour...Shut your

eyes very tight, and then we can all see. I wonder what our eyes and nose will tell us…" Wait. Remove the cloth over the raised batch so children can see it.

"I wonder how this yeast made the flour so big…If the flour is the world, I wonder what the yeast really is…"

"I wonder how the kingdom of God is like the yeast mixed into flour…"

Prayer:
"If you would like to say something to God, you may say it now." Wait. Listen to the children's prayers. Then pray, "Dear God, thank you for bringing your kingdom to the whole world!"

Worship Song:
"O Magnify the Lord."

Conclusion/Transition:
"You may put all of these dishes onto the dishwashing table if you would like to wash them. I will fold the mixing cloth and put it into the laundry.

"You may get a bucket, sponge, and water to wipe the table. If you see flour on the floor, you may sweep it up with the broom and dustpan." (I privately will bake the bread but will not tell the children as that will not fit with the dynamics of the parable.)

Indirect Purpose:
To marvel at the great plan of God for goodness and grace in this world.

Philosophy:
To wonder and admire how great the kingdom of God really can become as compared with its beginning.

Lesson 19
The Lord's Supper, Part 1

Materials:

Two green circles (sheep fold and pasture), Good Shepherd, ten sheep, table, small tablecloth, bread, plate for bread, and cup.

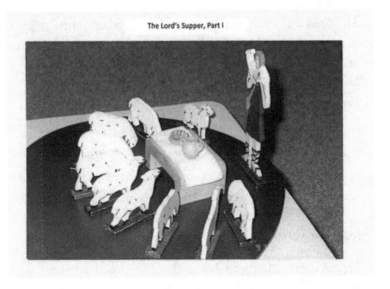

The Lord's Supper, Part I

Reading of Scripture:
Matthew 26:26-29.

Purpose:
To show the children that the Good Shepherd loves the sheep so much that He includes them in His special feast covenant.

Presentation:

1. Place the ten sheep inside the sheepfold, standing, and the Good Shepherd at the door of the fold. Say, "We remember the Good Shepherd and His sheep. The sheep have rested safely at night, and the Good Shepherd says, 'I have prepared a special feast for you. Come with me to the table.'

2. "The Good Shepherd leads the sheep out to the pasture. He invites them to the feast, saying, 'Come to the table that I have prepared for you.'" Say, "He calls their names, each one, and they follow Him. He loves them so much, and they love Him. They

are so happy to be with Him!"

3. All ten sheep come in a semi-circle to the front of the table. The Good Shepherd stands behind the table. He lays out the cloth, the plate, the bread, and the cup.

4. Say, "The Good Shepherd took the bread, broke it" (pretend), "and said, 'Thank you, Father, for this bread and drink.' Then He said, 'This bread reminds you of my body that is broken for you for the forgiveness of your sins. Whenever you eat this bread, you remember me.'" Say, "He passes the bread to each sheep, and they take a bite.

5. "Then He takes the cup and says, 'This cup of drink reminds you of my blood that is poured out for you for the new promise. Drink this cup and remember me.'" He passes the cup to each sheep, and they all ten take a drink.

6. "Then He calls His sheep back to the fold, and they follow Him. They listen for His voice, and they know His voice. He says, 'I love you so much that I would even give my life for you.' They follow closely behind Him to the sheepfold because the way is narrow."

7. The narrative ends with the sheep back in the fold and the Good Shepherd at the door. The sheep lie down to rest for the night.

Meditation:
"I wonder what this all could mean...I wonder who the sheep really are...I wonder who the Good Shepherd really is...I wonder what kind of 'new promise' the Good Shepherd has for them..."

Prayer:

"If you would like to say something to the Good Shepherd, you may say it now." Wait. Then say, "Dear Good Shepherd, thank you for the special feast and new promise that you have given us. Amen."

Worship Song:
"Glorify Thy Name."

Conclusion/Transition:

"I will put this work away, and you may have a turn. It is a special lesson for you. I will help you if you need me."

Indirect Purpose:

To introduce children to the elements and the meaning of communion. To help them see the special feast and wonder if the sheep really are people and the Good Shepherd is Jesus.

Philosophy:

To discover that the sheep are really people and that the Good Shepherd is really Jesus Christ who gave us a new promise for eternal life.

Lesson 20
The Lord's Supper, Part 2

Materials:

Two circles, Good Shepherd, ten sheep, table, small table-cloth, bread, cup, ten modern figures, and Jesus figure.

Reading of Scriptures:
Matthew 26:26-29.

Direct Purpose:
To find out that the sheep actually are people, the Good Shepherd is Jesus, and the special feast and new promise is from Jesus to His people.

Presentation:

1. Begin the lesson with the sheep gathered at the pasture table and the Good Shepherd at the table as in "The Lord's Supper, Part 1."

2. Begin the following narrative, and as you speak, remove one sheep at a time to its basket and put out a US figure at the table.

3. Take the Good Shepherd away and put out the Jesus figure.

4. Say, "The Good Shepherd loves His sheep so much that, as we remember, He shares His special feast and new promise with them. Now we know that the sheep are people, and the Good Shepherd is Jesus. He has many flocks and many people that He loves. He will even give His life for them.

    Say the same words of the feast as you did in Part 1, and present the feast to the human figures as you did to the sheep, with Jesus presenting the special feast.

Meditation:
Wonderment:
"I wonder how the sheep could be people...I wonder how the Good Shepherd can become Jesus...I wonder what this all

could mean…"

Prayer:
"Close your eyes very tight. You may say something to Jesus if you like." Wait. Then say, "Dear Jesus, thank you for sharing your special feast and new promise with us. Amen."

Worship Song:
"Jesus, What a Wonder You Are."

Conclusion/Transition:
"I will put this very special work away, and you may have a turn. Perhaps you would like to use it with a friend…It is very special work. If you need a teacher's help, you may ask her."

Philosophy:

1. As the children use the lessons themselves, they will not remember everything to say, but if it is similar to the narrative, allow it.

2. In my first year of internship with children, we were using the Sunday school classroom for the Montessori school. (I don't recommend this when your husband is the pastor.) I had not taken the Cavalletti course yet but wanted to give the children an experience with Jesus that involved the senses. I gave the children a communion experience, and they enjoyed it. The children did not understand its true meaning, but they loved the prayer, the cracker, and the juice. Later a member of the elders found out and asked me not to do that again, that the children were not "of age." I suppose that is probably true, but I am now sure that the children understand the promise of love and care of the Good Shepherd (Jesus) from the table, cup,

and bread that we show today but are not yet aware of His death on the cross. Cavalletti did not share the death of Christ on the cross, either, by making material for the classroom. Young children should not be exposed to this very cruel death until later in their life.

3. One early morning a mother and daughter came to school, and the mother was crying. She took me aside and said that her husband had been drinking, his car left the road, and he was killed last night. I prayed with her, and we both cried, and she asked if her daughter could stay for the day anyway. I said, "Yes, of course," and that we had a lesson on "The Forever Life" that we would show her daughter. The daughter was only four and did not really understand what had happened, but, nevertheless, the teacher of that class showed the child the lesson. Amazingly, the teacher told me, the child used "The Forever Life" lesson three or four times before putting it away.

Indirect Purpose:
To show children that Jesus is the one who loves their family so much and gives them, both children and adults, the special feast and new promise.

Lesson 21
The Lord's Supper, Part 3

Materials:
Tray with table and tablecloth, a basket of international figures, basket of modern figures, loaf of bread, jug, table with cloth, and Jesus figure.

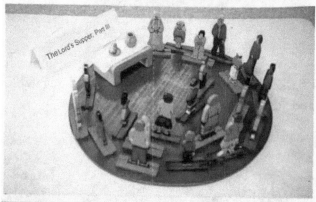

Reading of Scripture:
Matthew 28:19-20 (NIV), "Therefore go and make disci-
ples of all nations, baptizing them in the name of the Father

and of the Son and of the Holy Spirit and teaching them to obey everything I have commanded you."

Direct Purpose:
To let children know that God gives His children power and the right to go into all of the world and tell of His great love.

Presentation:

1. Take out the US figures from the Lord's Supper Part 2, and place them around the edge of the green wooden circular "pasture," also placing the table at the front edge with the cloth, bread, cup, and the Jesus figure in front.

2. Take the basket of international figures and place them around the edge of the pasture, placing both children and adults and US and international figures between each other. As you do, say, "Jesus has many flocks and many of His people all around the world. He loves them all so much!"

   Continue the narrative of Jesus' words of love to all people as you put out the figures.

3. With Jesus standing at the front, behind the table, say, "Jesus said, 'I have many flocks and many people to bring into my fold.'" Then sing, "We Are One in the Spirit."

   Say, "Jesus said to them, 'Go into all of the world and preach the Good News of God's love. Wait here until the Spirit of God comes upon you.'" Then say, "Jesus said, 'I choose, you, the pastor, to lead the church.'" Move a male figure behind the table. "Then Jesus says, 'I must go to be with my Father in heaven.'" Say, "And then Jesus left to go back to heaven." Move the figure of Jesus directly up and (mysteriously) away into the basket.

Say, "The pastor says, 'Thank you, dear God, for our Lord Jesus Christ, and for this special celebration Jesus has given us. Let us celebrate! When our Lord was here, He took bread and broke it and said, "This bread reminds you of my body, broken for you. Eat of it."'" The pastor passed it out to all of the people, and they ate.

4. Then say, "The pastor then took the cup and said, 'This drink reminds you of Jesus' blood that was poured for you for the forgiveness of your sins. It is a new promise to you forever.' He passed it out to all of his people, and they drank it."

5. Say, "Then God sent His Spirit upon all of the people. The people worshipped God and spoke many languages. They were filled with God's Spirit." (Blow a great wind, and then lay down each person upon the circle, face down.)

6. Then stand the people up and move the pastor to the edge of the circle to lead the people out to the world, and say, "The pastor said, 'Jesus said, "Go, into the world and tell all nations about me, baptizing them in the name of the Father, Son, and Holy Spirit." Come, follow me!'" Have the pastor lead them off the circle to the edge of the table.

Meditation:
Wonderment:
"I wonder what this all could mean...How would there be so many people at Jesus' table...How could people be from all over the world..."

Prayer:

"Would you like to say something to Jesus?" Wait. Listen to the children's prayers. Then say, "Dear God, please fill us with your Holy Spirit. Amen."

Worship Song:

"I Worship you, Almighty God."

Closing/Transition:

"I will put this work away, and you may have a turn. It is a big work, but I will help you if you need it. Please come and whisper in my ear what God tells you about this lesson."

Philosophy:

1. Remember that the Lord's Supper Part 3 really happened and could use realistic three-dimensional figures. It does use a three-dimensional figure of Jesus. The elements of communion are three-dimensional, as are many other objects in our parable stories, for the sake of convenience and realism.

2. We begin with parable sheep and continue with parable figures in these three lessons in order to link the three lessons.

3. Ask the Holy Spirit to give you wisdom and anoint you as you use these lessons with young children.

Indirect Purpose:

To inform children of the gift of the Holy Spirit and His command to go and tell the world of His love.

Lesson 22
The Ten Young Maidens

Materials:

Parable house, five figures of young women carrying lamps and oil, five figures of young women with lamps but no extra oil, and figure of bridegroom in a gold robe.

Reading of Scripture:
Matthew 25:1-13.

Age:
Four years and up.

Direct Purpose:
To let children know that Jesus will be back someday soon and we can have faith as we wait for Him.

Presentation:

1. "Jesus said, 'I will tell you another kingdom of heaven story: Once there were ten young women who took their oil lamps and went out to meet the bridegroom. Five of them were foolish, and five of them were wise. The five that were foolish took their lamps but did not take any extra oil with them, while the wise ones took containers full of oil for their lamps.'"

2. Say, "A friend of theirs was getting married that evening, and it was the job of the ten ladies to provide light on the pathway to the wedding place.'" (There were no lamps lit along the way.)
   Show the ten ladies moving along the road in two lines toward the parable house. They arrived and waited outside for the bridegroom to arrive.

3. "'The bridegroom was late, so the ladies began to nod and fall asleep.'" *Lay the two groups of five down on the ground to sleep.*

4. "'It was already midnight when the cry rang out, 'The bridegroom is coming! Come and meet him!'"

5. "'The ten young women woke up and trimmed their lamps (turned them on).'" (Wake up all ten onto their feet.) "'The foolish ones said to the wise ones, "Let us have some of your oil because our

lamps are going out."

"No, indeed," the wise ones answered. "There is not enough for both you and us. Go to the store and buy some for yourselves."

6. "'So the foolish ones went off to buy some oil for themselves.'"

   Move the five foolish women away from the house to buy some oil. While they were gone, the bridegroom arrived.

7. Say, "'The five that were ready went in with Him to the wedding feast, and the door was shut.'"

   Move the five wise women out to meet the bridegroom and to follow him into the house.

8. "'Later the others arrived.'" (Show the five women going up to the door and knocking.) ""'Sir, sir, let us in!" they cried out.'"

   Show the bridegroom from inside, saying, "'Certainly not, I don't know you,' the bridegroom answered.

9. "And Jesus concluded, 'Watch out, then, for you do not know the day or the hour.'"

Meditation:

"I wonder who the wise and foolish women are...I wonder who the bridegroom is...I wonder what this wedding really is...I wonder what the oil really is...I wonder why the bridegroom would not open the door for the foolish women..."

Prayer:

"Would you like to say something to Jesus?" Wait. Then say, "Dear Jesus, thank you for your Holy Spirit that lives within us."

Worship Song:
"Worthy, Worthy, Worthy Is the Lamb" (Jesus).

Conclusion/Transition:
"I will put this work away, and you may have a turn. Maybe you will find out who the bridegroom really is...Maybe you will find out why the foolish ladies were turned away from the door...Maybe you can find out how we can get oil..."

Indirect Purpose:
To let the children know they are to be watching and preparing for the return of Jesus.

Philosophy: To prepare the children, as they learn more, to understand the consequences of our choices.

Lesson 23
The Wedding Garment

Materials:

Parable house, two king's servants, table and food items, son in a gold robe, ten good and bad street people with wedding garments, and man without wedding garment.

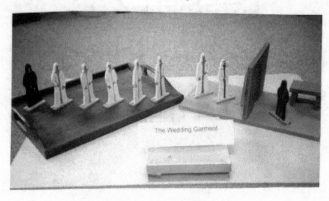

The Wedding Garment

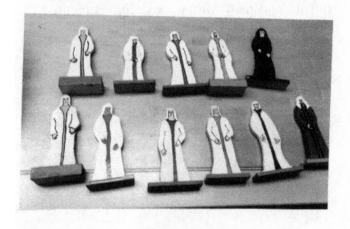

Reading of Scripture:
Matthew 22:1-14 (not for young children due to the violence).

Prerequisites:
Parable of leaven and parable of the mustard seed (histor-

ical parables).

Age:
Twelve years through adult.

Direct Purpose:
To show God's unrelenting call to us through church history and that we must respond with faith when He invites us.

Presentation:

1. "Jesus told another parable about the kingdom of heaven: 'Once there was a king who prepared a wedding feast for his son. He sent his servants to tell the invited guests to come to the feast, but they did not want to come. He sent other servants with this message for the guests: "My feast is now ready. The steaks and feast are prepared for you. Come to the wedding feast!" But the invited guests paid no attention and went about their business. One went to his farm and another to his store, while others grabbed, beat, and killed the servants.

2. "'The king was very angry,'" *so he sent his soldiers who killed those murderers and burned down their city.* (We do not show this episode to children until they are over five years of age.) Then he called his servants and said to them, "My wedding feast is ready, but the people that I invited did not deserve it. Now go to the main street and invite to the feast as many people as you find."

3. "'The servants went out into the streets and gathered all the people they could find, good and bad alike, and the wedding hall was filled with people.

4. "'The king went in to look at the guests and saw a man who was not wearing wedding clothes. "Friend, how did you get in here without wedding clothes?" the king asked him. But the man said nothing. Then the king told the servants, "Tie him up, hand and foot, and throw him out into the dark. There he will cry and gnash his teeth.'"

5. "And Jesus concluded, 'Many are invited, but few are chosen.'"

Meditation:
"I wonder what this all could mean…I wonder why the people that the king invited would not come to the feast…I wonder why it was so important to the king that the wedding hall be filled…I wonder what a wedding garment is and where you would get it…I wonder what it means if the king provided you a wedding garment, but you refused to wear it to the wedding…"

Prayer:
"Would you like to say something to God?" Wait. Listen to the children's prayers. Say, "Dear God, thank you for inviting me to your son's wedding feast. I will come."

Worship Song:
"I Worship You, Almighty God."

Conclusion/Transition:
"I will put this work away, and you may have a turn. Please come and whisper in my ear if you find out more about it."

Indirect Purpose:
To let the older children know what has previously happened in church history and that God will one day call them

to put on their wedding garment of faith and to come to the wedding feast of His Son.

Philosophy:
To rejoice that we all will receive a white wedding garment for the banquet in heaven.

Lesson 24
The Door

Materials:
Parable house, figure of Jesus, figure of a man, tablecloth, and small food, two chairs to fit the table.

Reading of Scripture:
Revelation 3:20.

Age:
Five years of age and up.

Prerequisite:

The two Good Shepherd parables and five infancy narratives.

Direct Purpose:

To show children the invitation of Jesus Christ to open the door of their heart and let Him come into their lives and live within them.

Presentation:

1. "Jesus said, 'Behold, I stand at the door of your heart and knock.'" Show the man at the table *inside the house.*

2. "If anyone hears my voice: 'Friend, I am here, at your door, ready to come into you...'" (*Show the Jesus figure knocking on the door.*)

3. "...I will come into him and eat with him and he with me." Show the man opening the door and the Jesus figure coming in. The two sit by the table and eat the food together. Show the man offering the food to Jesus, and they both eat it.

Meditation:
Wonderment:

"I wonder why Jesus stands at the door of our hearts and knocks...I wonder why He wants to come in...I wonder if He eats with us and if He will be there forever...I wonder what I need to say to Him to ask Him in..."

Prayer:

"If you would like to say something to Jesus, you may do it now. If you would like to ask Jesus to come into your heart, put your hand over your heart and knock on it. You may say, 'Jesus, please come in.' Dear God, We give thanks to you for sending us your Son to come live within us. Amen."

Worship Song:
"Amazing Grace."

Conclusion/Transition:
"Now that you asked Jesus to come into your heart, He lives within you. You may feel a special joy and wholeness, but perhaps you will not feel anything. It is very important to do four things: 1. Tell someone special in your life what decision you made. 2. Begin reading the Word of God in the New Testament, in the book of Mark. 3. Ask a pastor or another believer to baptize you with water and pray for you. 4. Find a good church and begin attending it. Feelings of joy and happiness will surely come to you!"

Philosophy:

1. Five-year-old children can decide to open the door of their heart to Jesus. My own children did. This Scripture makes it easy to realize that Jesus wants to come and live within us and enjoy life with Him.

2. Perhaps at a second time when this lesson is given after the children have heard it once, you can say this at the end, "If you want to ask Jesus to come into your heart today, you may lay your left hand over your chest where your heart is. I will come and knock on your hand and speak your name. You may say, 'Yes, Jesus, come into my heart and live with me.' We will then all pray together and thank Him for coming in."

3. Then sing the worship song, "Amazing Grace" (one verse).

Indirect Purpose:

To make it perfectly clear that we can invite Jesus into our lives, and He will never leave us. He will be with us and take care of us forever.

Lesson 25
The Great
Commandment

Materials:

Bible, heart-shaped basket of ten whole heart command-ments with numbers on them (1-10, not cut as a puzzle), fig-ure of Jesus, small zip-lock bag with the Ten Commandments written out in ten pieces, the first four in blue letters and the last six in red letters, and the words of Jesus written out in a long strip of blue ("Love the Lord your God with all of your heart, with all your soul, and with all your mind"), and in red ("and love your neighbor as yourself").

Reading of Scripture:
Mark 12:28.
Age:
Two and a half to six.

Prerequisite:
The Ten Commandments, Lesson 13.

Direct Purpose:
To know that the Ten Commandments can be divided into two different kinds.

Presentation:

1. "Someone asked Jesus, 'Which of all of the commandments is the most important?'

2. "Jesus answered, 'Love the Lord your God with all of your heart, with all of your soul, with all of your mind, with all of your strength, and love your neighbor as yourself.' These are the great commandments."

3. Say, "I will show you something!" Lay out the figure of Jesus at the top of the table, then the Bible, then lay out the two long strips of commandments, cut in half. The one about God must be on the left, and the one about people must be on the right.

4. Then lay out the ten whole heart-shaped cards of the commandments, in mixed order, onto the table.

5. Sort them by color, and lay them beneath the two strips in numerical order: 1-4 and 5-10.

Meditation:

Wonderment:

"There are many commandments. We remember that commandments are God's secrets to us for a happy life. I wonder which one will be the hardest to do? Which one will be the easiest?"

Prayer:

"If you would like to say something to God, you may say it now." Wait. Listen to the children pray. Say, "Dear God, thank you for these two great secrets for a happy life. We will follow your directions. Amen."

Worship Song:

"How I Love Your Law, O Lord!"

Conclusion/Transition:

To help the children investigate the meaning of the Great Commandments and the Ten Commandments.

Child and Faith Materials and Lessons

How to Make Figures

Parable Figures:

1. Use ¼" plywood and trace the figures from these diagram sheets.

2. Use a jigsaw or laser cutter to make parable figures.

3. Sand edges and dust figures.

4. Skin: Natural wood except for some international figures (or to your own choice).

5. Good Shepherd: Dark brown garment; light brown bag; light brown hair; black shoes; dark brown shoelaces; and natural wood for the skin.

6. Sheep: White.

7. Bases: Use a long strip of ¼" plywood.
   Make X" width x 1/8" depth. Make the length of the strip groove and cut 70 bases. (Adjust the length for wider figures.) Paint bases green, and glue the figures into the base.

8. After sanding and dusting the figures, paint the base wood with a base coat like Testor or some other enamel paint. Then use colored craft paint usually used for miniature cars for the figures.

9. Give a clear coat of paint or shellac (or Testor) over all sides but not the bottom.

Comet Star:

1. Cut a 1/4" piece of good quality plywood into a comet star (see diagram).

2. Sand, then paint it with shiny silver paint on both sides and edges.

3. Mount this comet star on a nail and insert it into a hole in the manger roof. (Or buy a large silver star and hang it onto a nail in the manger roof.) Do not remove string during the lesson.

4. Use a piece of dental floss for the comet string.

SHEEP

BASE

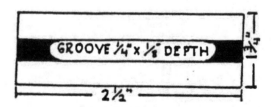

GROOVE ¼" x ⅛" DEPTH

2½"

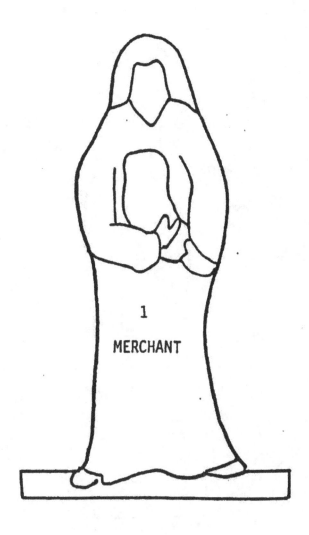

1

MERCHANT

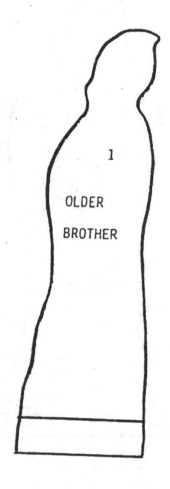

1

OLDER

BROTHER

THE FOUND SON

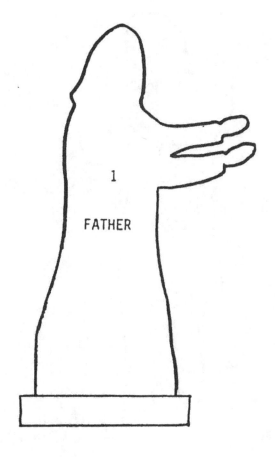

1

FATHER

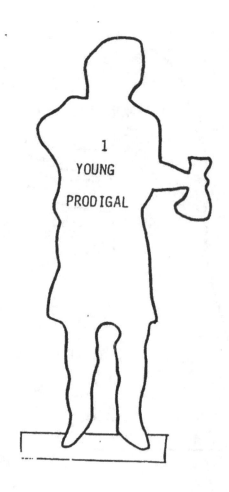

1
YOUNG
PRODIGAL

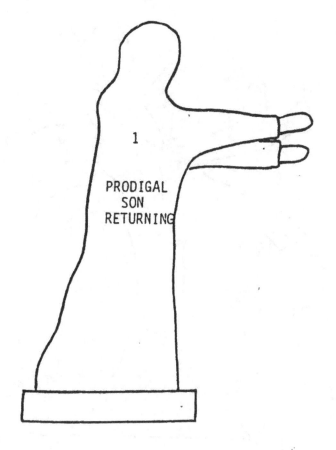

1

PRODIGAL
SON
RETURNING

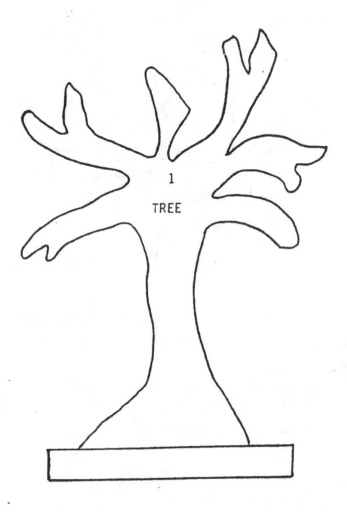

1

TREE

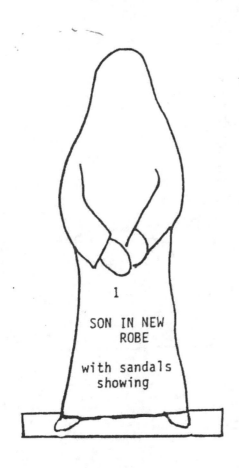

1

SON IN NEW
ROBE

with sandals
showing

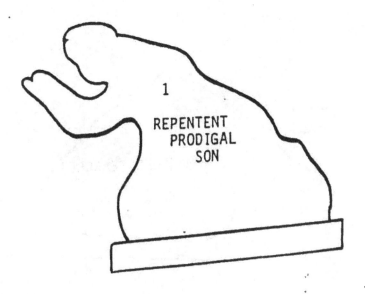

1

REPENTENT
PRODIGAL
SON

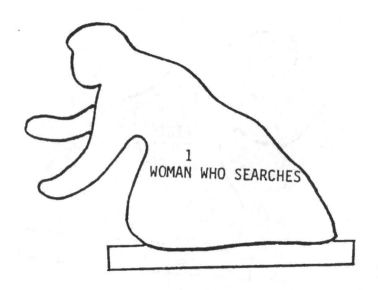

1
WOMAN WHO SEARCHES

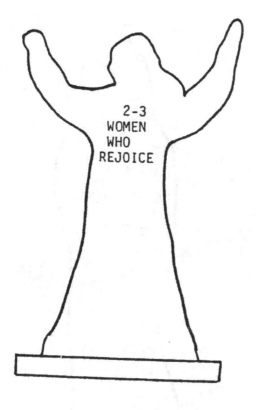

2-3
WOMEN
WHO
REJOICE

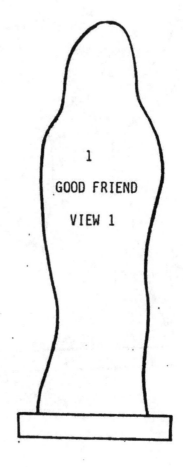

1

GOOD FRIEND

VIEW 1

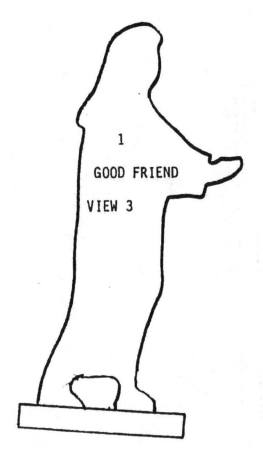

1

GOOD FRIEND

VIEW 3

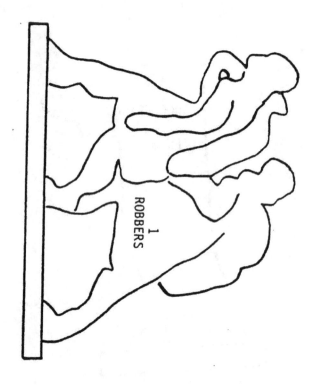

ROBBERS
1

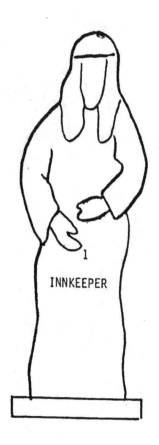

1

INNKEEPER

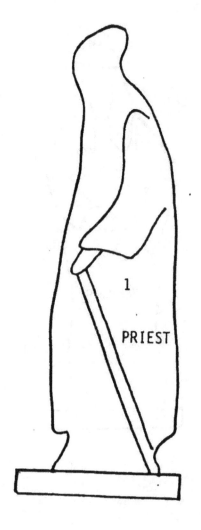

1

PRIEST

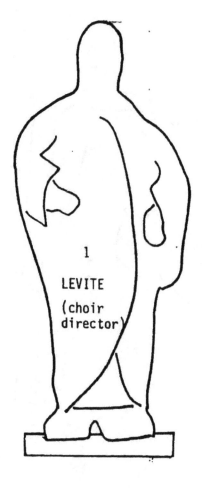

1

LEVITE

(choir
director)

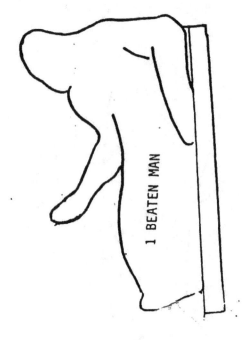

1 BEATEN MAN

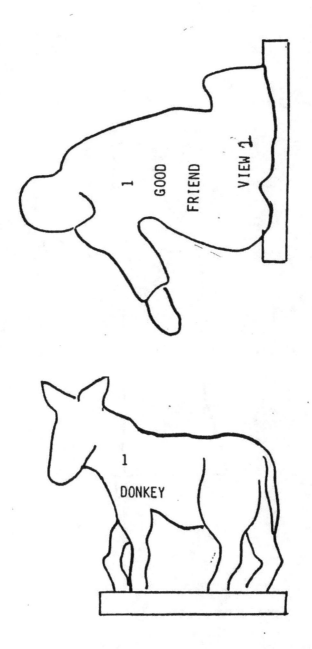

GOOD FRIEND

VIEW 1

1

DONKEY

1

1
WIFE

1

FRIEND
WHO HAS
BREAD

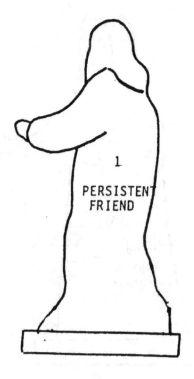

1
PERSISTENT
FRIEND

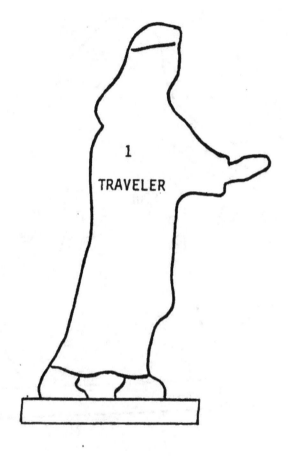

1

TRAVELER

SOWER

1

1

BRIDEGROOM

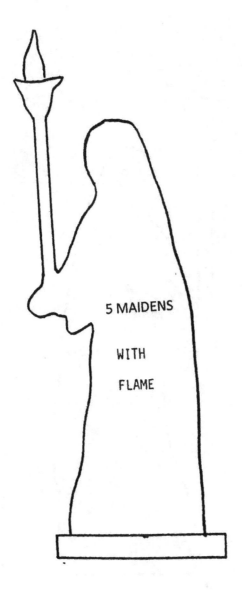

5 MAIDENS

WITH

FLAME

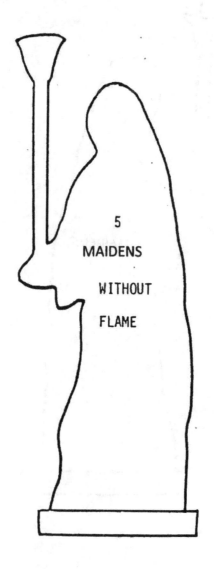

5

MAIDENS

WITHOUT

FLAME

WCU

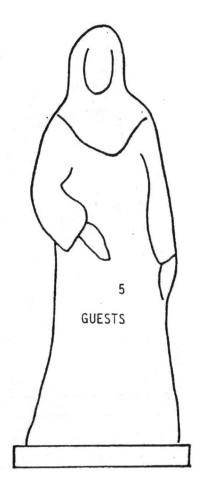

5

GUESTS

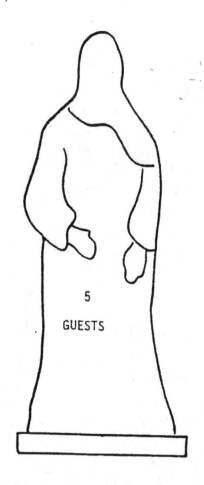

5

GUESTS

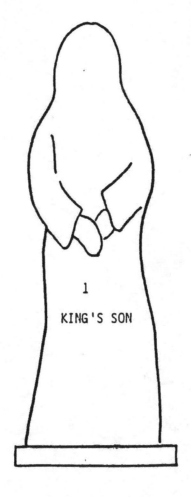

1

KING'S SON

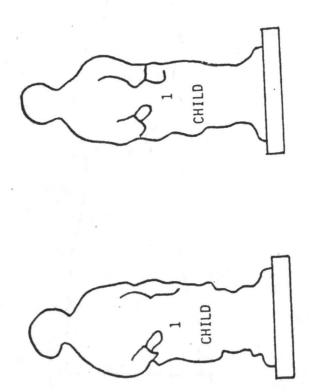

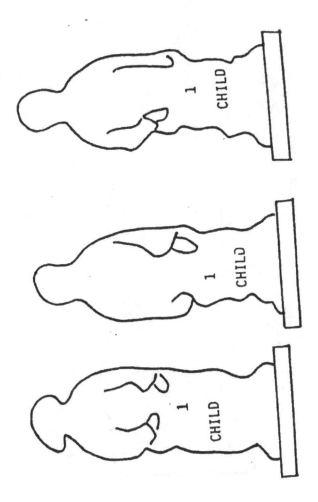

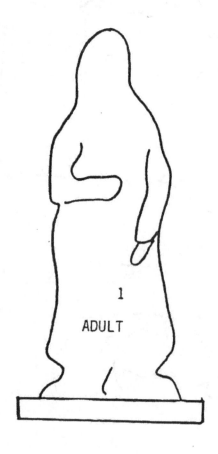

1

ADULT

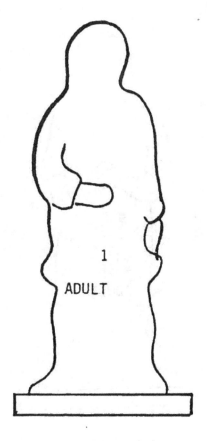

1
ADULT

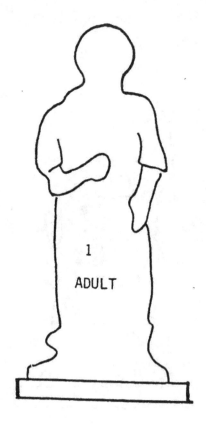

1

ADULT

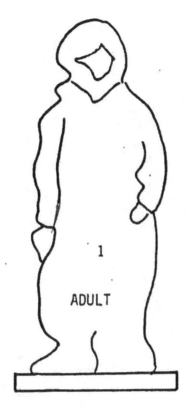

1

ADULT

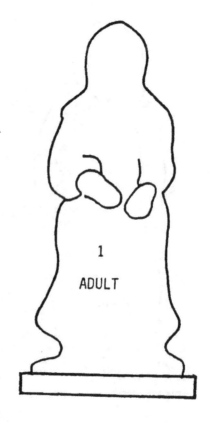

1

ADULT

Comet Star -

mounted on nail to be inserted
into hole in roof

Gifts - 3 small decorative gold or silver containers
(these may be found where miniatures or doll house items
are sold)

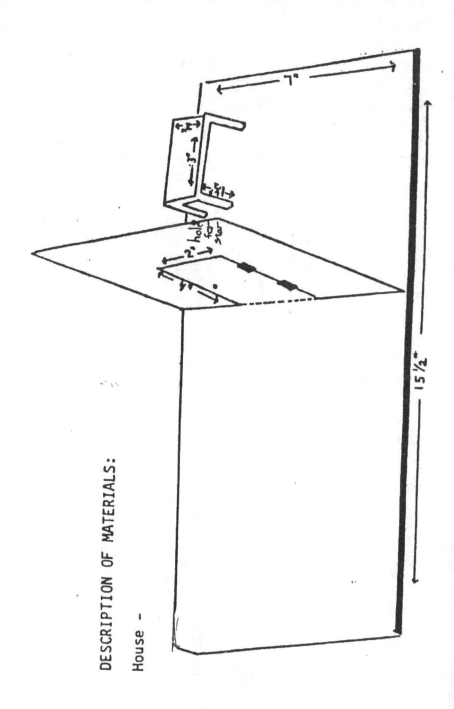

DESCRIPTION OF MATERIALS:

House –

CPSIA information can be obtained
at www.ICGtesting.com
Printed in the USA
FSHW010643190122

9 781637 696262